ASPEN PUBLISHERS

Strategies & Tactics for the MPRE

Multistate Professional Responsibility Exam

This edition revised by
Alex Ruskell
Associate Director of Academic Support
Roger Williams School of Law

Prior editions by
Lazar Emanuel, J.D.
Kimm Alayne Walton, J.D.

 Wolters Kluwer
Law & Business

AUSTIN   BOSTON   CHICAGO   NEW YORK   THE NETHERLANDS

Printed in the United States of America

1 2 3 4 5 6 7 8 9 0

ISBN 978-07355-7897-5

This book is intended as a general review of a legal subject. It is not intended as a source of advice for the solution of legal matters or problems. For advice on legal matters, the reader should consult an attorney.

About Wolters Kluwer Law & Business

Wolters Kluwer Law & Business is a leading provider of research information and workflow solutions in key specialty areas. The strengths of the individual brands of Aspen Publishers, CCH, Kluwer Law International and Loislaw are aligned within Wolters Kluwer Law & Business to provide comprehensive, in-depth solutions and expert-authored content for the legal, professional and education markets.

CCH was founded in 1913 and has served more than four generations of business professionals and their clients. The CCH products in the Wolters Kluwer Law & Business group are highly regarded electronic and print resources for legal, securities, antitrust and trade regulation, government contracting, banking, pension, payroll, employment and labor, and healthcare reimbursement and compliance professionals.

Aspen Publishers is a leading information provider for attorneys, business professionals and law students. Written by preeminent authorities, Aspen products offer analytical and practical information in a range of specialty practice areas from securities law and intellectual property to mergers and acquisitions and pension/benefits. Aspen's trusted legal education resources provide professors and students with high-quality, up-to-date and effective resources for successful instruction and study in all areas of the law.

Kluwer Law International supplies the global business community with comprehensive English-language international legal information. Legal practitioners, corporate counsel and business executives around the world rely on the Kluwer Law International journals, loose-leafs, books and electronic products for authoritative information in many areas of international legal practice.

Loislaw is a premier provider of digitized legal content to small law firm practitioners of various specializations. Loislaw provides attorneys with the ability to quickly and efficiently find the necessary legal information they need, when and where they need it, by facilitating access to primary law as well as state-specific law, records, forms and treatises.

Wolters Kluwer Law & Business, a unit of Wolters Kluwer, is headquartered in New York and Riverwoods, Illinois. Wolters Kluwer is a leading multinational publisher and information services company.

This book is dedicated to Jimmy and Mary Frances.

Table of Contents

Part One
Plan of Attack for the MPRE

A. Introduction

Along with graduating from law school and passing a state bar exam, you must pass the Multistate Professional Responsibility Examination (MPRE) if you want to practice law in most jurisdictions in the United States (all but four). The MPRE is designed to test your knowledge of two relatively short documents, the American Bar Association (ABA) Model Rules of Professional Conduct and the ABA Model Code of Judicial Conduct, as well as your "understanding of the generally accepted rules, principles, and common law regulating the legal profession in the United States."

The exam consists of 60 multiple-choice questions, 10 of which are not included in your final score (these are questions being tested by the examiners — you won't be able to tell the difference between a scored question and a test question). Each question has only one correct answer out of the four options.

The standard score scale ranges from 50 (low) to 150 (high). The conversion of your raw score (the number of questions you get right) to a scaled score (the score reported by the MPRE) involves a statistical process that adjusts for variations in the difficulty of different MPRE exams so that any particular scaled score will represent the same level of knowledge from test to test. For example, if a particular MPRE exam is considered easier than previous exams, the raw scores will be adjusted downward to account for this difference. The passing grade is different from state to state, but it is generally a scaled score between 70 and 86. To find the passing grade for your state, contact the state board of bar examiners.

By the time you finish your law school course in ethics or professional responsibility, you will have developed a general sense of the range of ethical problems lawyers face every working day. All you have to do to get past the MPRE is to apply this general sense to specific fact patterns created by the MPRE examiners.

Problems in legal ethics do not lend themselves easily to multiple choice questions. They are more logically dealt with in the essay format, which permits extensive discussion of alternatives and the statement of a nuanced conclusion. Believe it or not, this actually makes the MPRE a lot easier than most tests. There's a good reason for this — for a multiple-choice exam such as this one to be valid, the answers have to be *unquestionably* correct. Consequently, the MPRE won't use any multiple-choice question that could lead a test taker to conclude, "Well, the answer is A if you interpret it this way, and B if you interpret it this other way."

This simple fact — that each MPRE question has to have only one, indisputably correct answer — means that the questions and answers have to be written with especially broad strokes. In fact, MPRE questions and answers are written with such broad strokes that in a lot of cases you will be able to pick out the right answer at first glance. Consequently, the MPRE isn't particularly difficult, and with the advice in this book and a little extra preparation, you should pass it quite easily.

But, PEOPLE DO FAIL THE MPRE! You can't simply wander into the exam room on test day and hope for the best. Ultimately, there are two things that you need to do: one is to get familiar with the ethics rules, and the other is to get a sense of the kinds of questions that appear on the MPRE.

As you may know by now, the ABA Code and Rules are incredibly tedious to read. So, you'd be well advised to expand your preparation into a few more tools than simply trying to read the Code and Rules themselves. Along with this book, you should use the *Law in a Flash* card set on Professional Responsibility, which you will find at just about any law school bookstore. The flashcards offer more than 900 cards testing every aspect of the ABA Rules and Code. They define the basic rules and then give you hundreds of hypothetical fact patterns just like the ones tested on the MPRE. They have been revised and updated to reflect the most recent changes in the Model Rules of Professional Conduct and the Model Code of Judicial Conduct. The cards take only about 8–10 hours to review. They incorporate modern learning techniques that not only teach you the rules, but also how to apply those rules to facts quickly and effectively.

Of course, you can use any source to review the ethics rules, such as outlines or hornbooks. The point is that you have to *know* the rules. Other than that, you have to learn the structure and technique of MPRE questions, and that's what this book will show you. Part One shows you how to attack MPRE questions, and in Part Two, you'll get a chance to put this plan of attack into practice on some model MPRE Questions and Answers. In Part Three, you're completely on your own — Part Three contains

96 sample National Conference of Bar Examiners (NCBE) questions and the corresponding answer key. See if you can pick the right answer. If you read this book and put its plan of attack to work, you won't fail the MPRE unless you want to.

If you were expecting to review thousands of questions for the MPRE — relax. Part Two is made up of only 60 review questions because they do the whole job of teaching you how to deal with the structure of the exam.

Incidentally, all of the questions in this book — the ones used as examples in Part One, the model questions in Part Two, and the practice questions in Part Three — are real MPRE questions. They've all appeared on actual MPREs in prior years, and they're in this book courtesy of the NCBE. So you don't have to worry that the questions in this book may not resemble the ones you'll see on your MPRE — they were written by the very same people!

B. Basic Information About the MPRE

Background — The MPRE is created and administered by the NCBE, which is also responsible for the Multistate Bar Examination. The MPRE is currently administered in virtually every state, as well as the District of Columbia.

When Offered — The MPRE is administered three times a year — in March, August, and November. In many states, you can take the MPRE before you finish law school; in fact, you should take the MPRE as soon as you complete your course on Professional Responsibility, and take it early enough so that, if you do fail, you'll have another chance to take it before the bar exam (some states will not let you sit for the bar exam until *after* you have passed the MPRE).

Format and Length — The MPRE is made up of 60 multiple-choice questions, followed by ten questions that ask the test taker to evaluate the testing conditions of the exam. It lasts two hours and five minutes. It is similar to the Multistate Bar Examination in the sense that each question includes a fact pattern followed by four answer choices, from which you are supposed to choose the "best" response. Later in Part One, you'll see lots of examples of this question format, and you'll learn to analyze it down to its most essential elements.

Coverage — The MPRE covers the ABA Model Rules of Professional Conduct, as well as the ABA Model Code of Judicial Conduct. It doesn't attempt to cover the code of any individual state. (In actual practice you may find that the codes governing professional responsibility in your state differ in substantial respects from the ABA Rules and Code.)

The MPRE also tests the applicant's "understanding of the generally accepted rules, principles and common law regulating the legal profession"; in these items, the correct answer will be governed by the view reflected in the majority of cases, statutes, or regulations on the subject. In testing issues such as litigation sanctions or the attorney-client evidentiary privilege, the Federal Rules of Civil Procedure and the Federal Rules of Evidence apply.

The entire subject of legal malpractice, which is of vital concern to lawyers and which is tested on the MPRE, is not mentioned as such in the Model Rules.

Scoring — Your MPRE score is determined by how many questions you answer correctly; there's no penalty for incorrect answers. The lesson to be learned from this is that it pays to answer every question, even if you're not exactly sure what the correct answer is.

How to Apply for the MPRE — To apply for the MPRE, write or call:

> National Conference of Bar Examiners
> MPRE Application Department
> 301 ACT Dr.
> P.O. Box 4001
> Iowa City, IA 52243-4001
> Phone Number: (319) 341-2500

C. What the MPRE Tests

Scope of Questions

Questions on the ABA Model Rules and related sources dealing with the conduct of lawyers and law firms make up 90–94 percent of all the questions on the MPRE. The remaining questions test the applicant's knowledge of the Model Code of Judicial Conduct.

The outline of subjects published by the NCBE lists the items tested. Occasionally, other items are added, but the NCBE's outline is a good guide to the weight you should give each subject as you study. Not all of the items are tested each time, but if you've covered them all in your studies, you can't miss.

The NCBE's outline of MPRE subjects, and the approximate weight given to each, follows:

I. Regulation of the Legal Profession (6–12 percent)

  A. Powers of Courts and Other Bodies to Regulate Lawyers

  B. Admission to the Profession

  C. Regulation after Admission — Lawyer Discipline

  D. Mandatory and Permissive Reporting of Professional Misconduct

  E. Unauthorized Practice of Law — by Lawyers and Non-Lawyers

  F. Multi-Jurisdictional Practice

  G. Fee Division with a Non-Lawyer

  H. Law Firm and Other Forms of Practice

  I. Responsibilities of Partners, Managers, Supervisory, and Subordinate Lawyers

  J. Restrictions on Right to Practice

II. The Client-Lawyer Relationship (10–16 percent)

  A. Formation of Client-Lawyer Relationship

  B. Scope, Objective, and Means of the Representation

  C. Decision-Making Authority — Actual and Apparent

  D. Counsel and Assistance Within the Bounds of the Law

  E. Termination of the Client-Lawyer Relationship

  F. Client-Lawyer Contracts

  G. Communications with the Client

  H. Fees

III. Client Confidentiality (6–12 percent)

  A. Attorney-Client Privilege

  B. Work Product Doctrine

  C. Professional Obligation of Confidentiality — General Rule

  D. Disclosures Expressly or Impliedly Authorized by Client

  E. Other Exceptions to the Confidentiality Rule

IV. Conflicts of Interest (12–18 percent)

    A. Current Client Conflicts — Multiple Clients and Joint Representation

    B. Current Client Conflicts — Lawyer's Personal Interest or Duties

    C. Former Client Conflicts

    D. Prospective Client Conflicts

    E. Imputed Conflicts

    F. Acquiring an Interest in Litigation

    G. Business Transactions with Clients

    H. Third-Party Compensation and Influence

    I. Lawyers Currently or Formerly in Government Service

    J. Former Judge, Arbitrator, Mediator, or Other Third-Party Neutral

V. Competence, Legal Malpractice, and Other Civil Liability (6–12 percent)

    A. Maintaining Competence

    B. Expediting Litigation

    C. Candor to the Tribunal

    D. Fairness to Opposing Party and Counsel

    E. Impartiality and Decorum of the Tribunal

    F. Trial Publicity

    G. Lawyer as Witness

VI. Litigation and Other Forms of Advocacy (10–16 percent)

    A. Meritorious Claims and Contentions

    B. Expediting Litigation

    C. Candor to the Tribunal

    D. Fairness to Opposing Party and Counsel

    E. Impartiality and Decorum of the Tribunal

    F. Trial Publicity

    G. Lawyer as Witness

VII. Transactions and Communications with Persons Other than Clients (2–8 percent)

    A. Truthfulness in Statements to Others

    B. Communications with Represented Persons

    C. Communications with Unrepresented Persons

    D. Respect for Rights of Third Persons

VIII. Different Roles of the Lawyer (4–10 percent)

    A. Lawyer as Advisor

    B. Lawyer as Evaluator

    C. Lawyer as Negotiator

    D. Lawyer as Arbitrator, Mediator, or other Third-Party Neutral

    E. Prosecutors and Other Governmental Lawyers

    F. Lawyer Appearing in Non-Adjudicative Proceeding

IX. Safekeeping Funds and Other Property (2–8 percent)

    A. Establishing and Maintaining Client Trust Accounts

    B. Safekeeping Funds and Other Property of Clients

    C. Safekeeping Funds and Other Property of Third Persons

    D. Disputed Claims

X. Communication About Legal Services (4–10 percent)

    A. Advertising and Other Public Communications About Legal Services

    B. Solicitation — Direct Contact with Prospective Clients

    C. Group Legal Services

    D. Referrals

    E. Communications Regarding Fields of Practice and Specialization

XI. Lawyers' Duties to the Public and the Legal System (2–4 percent)

    A. Voluntary Pro Bono Service

    B. Accepting Appointments

    C. Serving in Legal Services Organizations

D. Law Reform Activities Affecting Client Interests

E. Criticism of Judges and Adjudicating Officials

F. Political Contributions to Obtain Engagements or Appointments

G. Improper Influence on Government Officials

H. Assisting Judicial Misconduct

XII. Judicial Ethics (2–8 percent)

A. Maintaining the Independence and Impartiality of the Judiciary

B. Performing the Duties of Judicial Office Impartially, Competently, and Diligently

C. Ex Parte Communications

D. Disqualification

E. Extra-Judicial Activities

D. Attacking the MPRE

1. Getting Familiar with the Question Format

MPRE questions are arranged in this way: They start with a fact pattern set around a common problem in legal ethics. This is followed by the "call" of the question, which directs you to what point of ethics the examiners are trying to test you on. Finally, there are four answer options. You are expected to choose the one that best answers the call. Here's a typical example:

An attorney represented a buyer in a real estate transaction. Due to the attorney's negligence in drafting the purchase agreement, the buyer was required to pay for a survey that should have been paid by the seller. The attorney fully disclosed this negligence to the buyer, and the buyer suggested that he would be satisfied if the attorney simply reimbursed the buyer for the entire cost of the survey.

Although the buyer might have recovered additional damages if a malpractice action were filed, the attorney reasonably believed that the proposed settlement was fair to the buyer. Accordingly, in order to forestall a malpractice action, the attorney readily agreed to make the reimbursement. The attorney drafted a settlement agreement, and it was executed by both the attorney and the buyer.

Was the attorney's conduct proper?

(A) Yes, if the attorney advised the buyer in writing that the buyer should seek independent representation before deciding to enter into the settlement agreement.

(B) Yes, because the attorney reasonably believed that the proposed settlement was fair to the buyer.

(C) No, because the attorney settled a case involving liability for malpractice while the matter was still ongoing.

(D) No, unless the buyer was separately represented in negotiating and finalizing the settlement agreement.

In this question, the first and second paragraphs make up the fact pattern. The final sentence, "Was the attorney's conduct proper?" is the "call" of the question — it tells you specifically what to look for in the answer options. Items A through D are the "answer options." One of these is the best response, and the other three are "distracters" — basically, answer options that are trying to "distract" you away from the right one. (Incidentally, the best response is A.)

2. Reading the Fact Patterns

On the MPRE, you have two minutes to read each question, answer it, and move on. This means not only that you have to have a ready grasp of the ethics rules, but that you also must be able to read and respond quickly. Most of all, you need to know what to look for. The most important thing to keep in mind about the MPRE is that it's very limited in the range of questions that it can raise. As with all standardized multiple-choice tests, the MPRE simply cannot test gray areas; the facts must clearly point toward one and only one correct answer for the question to be "psychometrically" sound — that is, for the question to be a valid measure of competence. In other words, there can't be a reasonable argument about which answer is the right answer.

Ultimately, although the examiners may be knowledgeable and crafty, there are only so many fact patterns they can concoct. They are testing you and every other law student in the country on your knowledge of the ethical rules, and they need to make sure that you understand the most important ones and follow them in your later practice. Consequently, in making the exam, they don't try to find the most obscure point or comment in the Rules simply to trick you. In many ways, the MPRE is more similar to a driving test than a typical law school exam.

In a driving test, the test-maker's goal is to make sure you know what a stop sign means, not what the paint on the sign is made from. What this means in practical terms is best shown by example.

Let's say that you and your best friend study for the MPRE together, and you both have an equally detailed knowledge of the rules of ethics; in fact, your knowledge of the rules is identical. For any given question on the MPRE to be valid as a testing device, you would both have to choose the same answer when confronted by any particular question. If you *didn't,* the question cannot be said to have tested your knowledge. Because you both had the same knowledge of the rules, the facts and the questions should have led you to the same result. If you each answered differently, and if this one question were the difference between passing and failing the MPRE, one of you would pass and the other would fail, *even though your knowledge of the rules was identical.* From the examiners' point of view, this would make the test invalid, because the test would fail its own purpose of distinguishing among students on the basis of their knowledge.

For instance, say a question involves a lawyer's representation of multiple parties who may have a conflict of interest. The issue is: Can the lawyer represent all of them in light of this potential conflict? Clearly, before a lawyer can properly ask the consent of the parties to a multiple representation, he or she must *reasonably believe* he or she can represent all the parties adequately. "Reasonableness" is a standard that is totally fact-dependent. Therefore, if the examiners wanted to test you on whether the lawyer *could* properly represent all the parties in this basic circumstance, they would have to write the question in one of two ways:

1. Make it unmistakably clear in the facts that the lawyer's belief was reasonable; or

2. Condition the propriety of the representation on facts raising the issue of reasonableness — for instance, by saying, "The representation is proper *if* the attorney reasonably believes he can adequately represent the parties and he obtains their fully informed consent."

If the examiner failed to use either of these options, the question would not be a valid test of the rule requiring consent in advance of all parties to a multiple-party representation. In fact, if a question that is offered on the MPRE doesn't "perform as intended" — a term describing an ambiguous question that sneaks by the drafting committee — it is dropped from the exam.

If this theory for testing the validity of a test question isn't all that clear to you now, don't worry. The only thing that really matters is that you appreciate its impact on what you should look for in MPRE fact patterns. Looking at some of these points individually may clarify matters.

a. Pay special attention to statements about the lawyer's or the client's state of mind

In many ethics rules, the propriety of a lawyer's conduct depends on whether he or she *knows* or *believes* something. His or her knowledge or belief will determine whether some act on his or her part is mandated or prohibited. Pay special attention to words or phrases like "knows," "knowingly," "concludes," "becomes convinced," "believes," and "reasonably believes." In fact, on many ethical issues, the attorney's belief about a fact or an event is more important than the fact or event itself.

Take a typical question about a lawyer's role in recommending a candidate for admission to the bar. According to the Rules, a lawyer cannot "***knowingly* make a false statement of material fact**" in connection with an applicant's admission to the bar. Model Rule 8.1.

Looking at the Rule carefully, you should notice that it doesn't matter whether the person the lawyer recommends later turns out to be a drug dealer; as long as *the lawyer didn't know the true facts* at the time he or she made the recommendation, he or she will not be subject to discipline.

Take another example — the problem of conflicts of interest. In most conflict cases, the conflict can be remedied by obtaining the informed consent of the affected clients whether they are prospective, current, or former clients. However, before the lawyer can even *seek* a client's consent, he or she must *reasonably believe* he or she can carry on the representation of that client without adverse affect on his or her representation of another client. Model Rule 1.7. Here again, it doesn't really matter whether his or her belief ultimately proves to be sound; as long as the lawyer *reasonably believed* at the time that he or she undertook the representation that he or she could do so without adversely affecting either party, the lawyer will not be subject to discipline.

The lesson here is that it's important to pay attention to the MPRE's description of the attorney's state of mind — i.e., his or her beliefs and knowledge — in determining whether or not he or she has acted ethically.

b. Pay attention to the lawyer's motivation when he or she acts or fails to act

Just as the extent of an attorney's knowledge can determine the propriety or impropriety of his or her behavior, so too can his or her reasons for undertaking, or failing to undertake, the behavior. You should always make special note of the reason for an attorney's actions. Often, that will help you in assessing the propriety of his or her conduct.

For example, on a question dealing with permissive or mandatory withdrawal from representation, the attorney's reasons for withdrawing will be crucial in determining whether or not the withdrawal is ethical. Some questions will raise obvious issues of motivation, but others will insert more insidious circumstances in which motivation may play a less obvious but equally critical role.

Take, for instance, whether to call a particular witness at trial. Ordinarily, whether or not to call a particular witness is the exclusive decision of the attorney, not the client. Model Rule 1.2. Under ordinary circumstances, the attorney has acted perfectly properly if he or she decides *not* to call a particular witness after careful deliberation.

But suppose he or she decides not to call a particular witness because it would take too much time and energy on his or her part to find and prepare the witness. Then his or her motives would raise issues both of incompetent representation under Model Rule 1.1, and of a lack of reasonable diligence under Model Rule 1.3. When the lawyer's behavior raises questions about his or her *motivation,* you have to analyze that motivation carefully to determine whether the behavior itself was proper.

c. Ignore "window dressing" — pay attention to the lawyer's core behavior

In some MPRE questions, the examiners test your knowledge of the ethical rules by surrounding unethical behavior with the "trappings" of propriety. This is to test whether you can tell the trees from the forest — that is, to see if you can find evidence of unethical conduct when it's surrounded by misleading "goodies."

For example, lawyers have a duty to provide competent service to their clients. Model Rule 1.1. A question that asked only, "Is a lawyer subject to discipline for providing incompetent service," free of other facts, wouldn't lead anyone into answering "No," however little the test-taker actually knew about the rules of ethics.

So this simple question, without more, wouldn't make a very good MPRE question. But suppose the lawyer *tells* the client that he is not competent to handle the matter, but the client insists that he handle it anyway, because the lawyer is the only lawyer she really trusts. Say also that the client is the lawyer's biggest client, and that the client says she will take her business elsewhere if the lawyer doesn't accept the matter. Now suppose that the client signs an affidavit acknowledging that the lawyer has advised her that he doesn't believe that he is skilled enough to handle the matter competently, and promising that she will not sue him for malpractice regardless of the outcome of the case. Even though the facts have been embellished, the "nub" of the matter is still the same — the lawyer is incompetent to handle the matter. Simply by adding seemingly relevant new facts — namely, the client's insistence on the lawyer's handling the work, her waiver of the right to competent represen-tation, and her agreement not to sue — a question that was too easy to use has been transformed into a more appropriate one.

Ultimately, the way to insulate yourself against the trap that's been set for you by these kinds of embellishments is to strip them all away and ask yourself what's really going on. Start with the undisputed fact that, underneath it all, the lawyer will provide incompetent service. Then work your way up from there to see if any of the additional facts — here, those additional facts are client consent and waiver — change the nature of that core issue. The answer here is "No." A lawyer who provides incompetent service cannot take comfort in client consent. The requirement of compe-tent representation is unqualified and inflexible.

If you maintain your focus in this way, you will make it extremely difficult for the examiners to confuse you by layering on facts that don't really change the underlying issue. In fact, the most common way that the examiners try to distract you from the right answer is to "fix" the Rule violation with a good outcome, client consent, or the fact that the attorney or judge would have done things the same way even if there was not a potential breach of ethics. Thus, always be wary of such "no harm, no foul" fact scenarios and answer options.

3. Reading the "Call" of the Question

The "call" of the question contains the instructions that you are expected to follow in choosing among the answers. The call flows logically from the facts, but it can take many forms. It can be very general — for instance, it can ask simply if the attorney's conduct was proper, improper, or subject to discipline — or it can be specific, inquiring into a particular aspect of the attorney's conduct.

a. "General" call

When a general call is used, the prevailing issue should spring to mind as you read the fact pattern. Here's an example:

> An attorney is a member of the bar and a salaried employee of the trust department of a bank. As part of his duties, he prepares a monthly newsletter concerning wills, trusts, estates, and taxes that the bank sends to all of its customers. The newsletter contains a recommendation to the customer to review his or her will in light of the information contained and, if the customer has any questions, to take the will to the bank's trust department where the trust officer will answer any questions without charge. The trust officer is not a lawyer. If the trust officer is unable to answer the customer's questions, the trust officer refers the customer to the attorney.
>
> Is the attorney subject to discipline for the foregoing?
>
> **(A)** Yes, because the attorney is giving legal advice to persons who are not his clients.
>
> **(B)** Yes, because the attorney is aiding the bank in the unauthorized practice of law.
>
> **(C)** No, because no charge is made for the attorney's advice.
>
> **(D)** No, because it is the attorney's duty to carry out the bank's instructions.

As you read this fact pattern, the one fact that should have popped out at you is that the attorney is helping a non-lawyer (the bank) to practice law. Consequently, the prime issue is the unauthorized practice of law.

If, for whatever reason, you have a problem spotting the issue in a "general call" question, try the following tactic: Rephrase the questions by turning it around. Here, you might ask yourself: "Why *shouldn't* the attorney be subject to discipline on these facts?" Or, "Why *would* he be?"

Take note: If a question asks you whether a particular act is unethical, you can be *pretty* sure that the attorney's done something that fits a particular clause of one of the ethics rules, or one of the exceptions to the rule, or that the conduct itself is unethical — otherwise, the question wouldn't be a very good testing item.

b. "Specific call"

Most MPRE questions call for more specific answers. For example: "Is it proper for the attorney to represent both parties in the contempt proceedings?" "Is the attorney subject to discipline if he asserts such a defense?" "Is it proper for the attorney to supply the judge with the requested list of writings on the subject of custody?" "Is it proper for the attorney to grant the extension of time without consulting the client?" Unlike a general call, the specific call will usually define the issue you're looking for. Looking at these particular calls more closely should help to clarify this point.

> "Is it proper for the attorney to represent both parties in the contempt proceedings?"

The issue here is almost certainly *conflict of interest,* because you're being asked whether it would be proper to represent two people in the same proceeding at the same time.

> "Is the attorney subject to discipline if he asserts such a defense?"

Here, the issue probably relates to frivolous claims or fraud. The Rules specify that an attorney shall not knowingly make a false statement of material fact or law to a tribunal. Model Rule 3.3. They also prohibit a lawyer from bringing or defending a proceeding unless there is a non-frivolous basis for doing so. Model Rule 3.1.

> "Is it proper for the attorney to supply the judge with the requested list of writings on the subject of custody?"

The issue here is obviously *ex parte* contact with judges.

> "Is it proper for the attorney to grant the extension of time without consulting the client?"

The issue is undoubtedly the relative control of the attorney and the client over the process of decision-making during the representation or trial. The issue is given away by the words *"without consulting the client."*

If you found this exercise difficult, it's probably because you aren't — not yet, anyway — sufficiently familiar with the Model Rules. Once you've learned them and how they relate to MPRE fact patterns, it will be easier for you to find the issues raised by the MPRE, especially when the call of the question is specific.

c. Spotting the issue when it's not obvious from the fact pattern

In either general or specific call questions, if you can't find the issue in the facts, study the answer options. They will usually give the issue away. Obviously, the right answer will suggest the issue, but at least one or two of the other answers may suggest it as well. That's because the examiners go to great lengths to craft some of the wrong answers as distracters. While these also point to or suggest the main issue, they manage to avoid it, however narrowly. Here's an example:

> A plaintiff and defendant are next-door neighbors and bitter personal enemies. The plaintiff is suing the defendant over an alleged trespass. Each party believes, in good faith, in the correctness of his position. After the plaintiff had retained an attorney, he told the attorney, "I do not want you to grant any delays or courtesies to the defendant or his lawyer. I want you to insist on every technicality."
>
> The attorney has served the defendant's attorney with a demand to answer written interrogatories. The defendant's attorney, because of the illness of his secretary, has asked the attorney for a five-day extension of time within which to answer them.
>
> Is the attorney subject to discipline if she grants the defendant's attorney's request for a five-day extension?
>
> **(A)** Yes, because the attorney is acting contrary to her client's instructions.
>
> **(B)** Yes, unless the attorney first informs the plaintiff of the request and obtains the plaintiff's consent to grant it.

(C) No, unless granting the extension would prejudice the plaintiff's rights.

(D) No, because the defendant's attorney was not at fault in causing the delay.

Look carefully at the language in the various answer options here: "granting the extension"; "... the plaintiff's consent"; "... client's instructions." All of them suggest that this is an inquiry into the relative decision-making roles of the lawyer and the client. The best response is C. Why? Because it recognizes that the underlying reason for assigning different levels of control over decision-making to the lawyer and the client *is to avoid prejudice to the client's basic rights.* At the same time, it recognizes that lawyers may take such action as is impliedly authorized to carry out representation and that clients normally defer to the special knowledge and skill of their lawyer regarding technical and tactical issues during litigation. Model Rule 1.2, Comments [1] and [2]. The other options are skillful distracters. Answer A suggests that a lawyer always has to get his or her client's consent on issues of litigation tactics. This is not the case. Answer B is wrong for the same reason as A. Answer D is easy to eliminate. The issue is whether a delay would prejudice the plaintiff's rights, regardless of what caused the delay. Whether the defendant's attorney was at fault in causing the delay is immaterial to the attorney's decision to grant the request for an extension.

4. Reading the Answers and Choosing the Best Response

As with any standardized test, the best — and sometimes the only — way to arrive at the best response is to eliminate all the options that are *definitely wrong.*

This means that the most important skill you can apply to the MPRE is the ability to perceive when an answer is definitely wrong. There are several ways to hone this skill:

- Learn the general principles for determining when an answer is wrong;

- Review the substantive rules that are most likely to trip you up;

- Learn the traps the examiners expect you to fall into; and

- Learn how to handle *modifiers.*

You'll learn all four of these skills in the next few pages. But one point you simply can't ignore is this — the most important element in your success is early and constant review of the Rules themselves. Unlike the LSAT and most other standardized exams, the MPRE is not a test of general intelligence or knowledge. It's based on your intimate knowledge of a specific set of rules which, stripped to their bare bones, cover less than 100 pages of text. That is, it's designed to test your knowledge of a limited subject, and you can't expect to pass it without having at least a reasonable familiarity with the Model Rules and the Model Code of Judicial Conduct. The advice on the next few pages assumes that you've already done your substantive review.

The instructions below will do two things for you. First, they'll ensure that you aren't tripped up by the MPRE's format, and that you'll always get the right answer if you know the rule. Also, these instructions will help you find your way to the right answer when you're not really sure what that answer ought to be. The bottom line is, if you are reasonably familiar with the ethics rules and you apply the principles in this chapter, *the* MPRE *cannot beat you!*

a. General principles of elimination

The most important skill you can take to the MPRE is the ability to identify when an answer is clearly wrong. What makes this more difficult than you may think is the extraordinary skill applied by the examiners in creating the wrong answers. Perhaps you've heard it said that you can tell the quality of a James Bond movie by watching the bad guy — the better the villain, the better the movie. Well, on standardized exams, the better the wrong answers, the more difficult the exam. The MPRE is difficult exactly because the examiners are exceptionally successful in masking the wrong answers to make them seem right. In this section, you'll learn how to "unmask" the wrong answers and make them easier to spot. Once you know how to eliminate the wrong answers with skill and confidence, you'll be able to pick out the *right* answer every time. Here, then, are the rules you need to know.

(1) If you know the right answer for sure, ignore these instructions.

If there is no question in your mind that one answer is correct, choose it and move on. If you've studied the substance of the Rules and read and practiced with this book, you should find the right answer on a first or second reading. If you do spot the right answer right away, mark your answer sheet and go on to the next question.

(2) Eliminate any answers you know are wrong, and then concentrate on the remaining answer choices.

In many cases you will immediately recognize that at least one and perhaps two of the answer choices are wrong. If you can spot three, great — you're left with the one option that has to be right. Don't bother to look a second time at answer options that are clearly wrong; cross them off in your test booklet if necessary to take your mind off them, and concentrate on the other possibilities.

(3) Remember that many of the answers will seem to draw on the same issue.

This rule isn't set in stone, but the nature of the exam makes it likely that several answers will focus on the same issue. Remember, what makes a standardized test difficult is the seeming resemblance between the *wrong* answers and the *right* one. This leads to one simple rule: *in general,* if there is a single answer option that seems very different from the other options, it's probably not the best answer. For example, if a multiple-choice exam was trying to test whether you knew that the sun was a star, and the answer options were "star," "nebula," "constellation," and "duck," you can generally get rid of "duck" immediately.

(4) Analyze the ways in which a particular answer can be wrong.

There are several clues to concluding that an answer is wrong. An answer is wrong if:

(a) It misapplies a rule of ethics to the facts. This is far and away the most common type of distracter; this will be discussed this in detail under "Traps Set by the Examiners."

(b) It misstates the ethics rules. This is also relatively common.

(c) It misstates or deliberately confuses the facts. An answer of this kind is so clearly wrong that it fools only the least prepared applicants; for this reason, it's not used very often.

b. A few general rules to remember

Here are a few general rules you should keep in mind. They will save you a lot of time in choosing the right answer.

(1) Don't be confused by a question that suggests that the lawyer's conduct, though questionable, has not prejudiced the client.

This is a very common MPRE trap — the facts describe conduct by a lawyer that is wrong, but then tell you that the misconduct has not affected the client adversely. When this happens in an MPRE fact pattern, you can bet your bottom dollar that at least one of the distracters will suggest that the lawyer's conduct was proper because his client wasn't "prejudiced," or "adversely affected," or the like. For this reason, it's important to keep the following basic rule in mind — even if things work out all right for the client, the lawyer may still be subject to discipline for violating the Rules in the first place. To avoid picking the wrong answer in this kind of question, you need to know the Model Rules in all their subtleties. (Note: *To recover in a malpractice case, the client has to show not only that the lawyer's conduct was negligent or improper, but that the conduct was the direct cause of the client's loss or injury.*)

For example, say a lawyer allows a paralegal in his office to conduct a deposition or perform some other act that constitutes the practice of law. The lawyer will be subject to discipline for assisting a person who is not a member of the bar in the unauthorized practice of law (Model Rule 5.5(a)) *even if* that person renders competent service. As another example, suppose a lawyer neglects the client's work over an extended period; he or she may be subject to discipline *even if* he or she finally manages to file the client's claim before the statute of limitations runs out.

The way to think of this behavior is that it is similar to the crime of burglary: once a person's broken into a dwelling at night with the intent to commit a felony therein, it doesn't matter what he or she does after that — he or she can change his or her mind and exit without touching anything — he or she is still guilty of burglary. It's the same with some lawyer infractions. Once a lawyer has engaged in unethical conduct, it doesn't really matter what the consequence of that conduct is to the client;

the lawyer has violated the ethics rules and he or she is subject to discipline.

(2) When it comes to fees, less is better

Occasionally the MPRE will ask about the propriety of a fee that is in dispute. Remember that the Model Rules specify that a lawyer's fee shall be reasonable (Model Rule 1.5(a)); it's a safe bet, therefore, that a lower fee will be perceived as more reasonable than a higher one. Thus, when a question asks what part of a fee a lawyer may properly keep, you're generally safe if you opt for the choice that best protects the client's interests in the money under dispute. Here's an example:

> A client retained an attorney to appeal the client's criminal conviction and to seek bail pending appeal. The agreed fee for the appearance on the bail hearing was $50 per hour. The attorney received $800 from the client, of which $300 was a deposit to secure the attorney's fee and $500 was for bail costs in the event that bail was obtained. The attorney maintained two office bank accounts: a "Fee Account," in which all fees were deposited and from which all office expenses were paid, and a "Client Fund Account." The attorney deposited the $800 in the "Client Fund Account" and expended six hours of time on the bail hearing. The effort to obtain bail was unsuccessful. Dissatisfied, the client immediately demanded return of the $800.

It is now proper for the attorney to:

(A) transfer the $800 to the "Fee Account."

(B) transfer $300 to the "Fee Account" and leave $500 in the "Client Fund Account" until the attorney's fee for the final appeal is determined.

(C) transfer $300 to the "Fee Account" and send the client a $500 check on the "Client Fund Account."

(D) send the client a $500 check and leave $300 in the "Client Fund Account" until the matter is resolved with the client.

With no other thought in mind than the general rule that "less for the lawyer, more for the client" is better than the alternative, you can see that the best response would have to be D, because it's the one in which the attorney gets to keep less than he does in any other response.

(3) If a rule forbids communication between two persons, it doesn't matter who initiates the communication.

The Model Rules contain many provisions that forbid communication between a lawyer and someone else. Examples: A lawyer shall not communicate with a person he or she knows to be represented by another attorney without that attorney's consent; a lawyer shall not communicate *ex parte* with a judge, juror, or prospective juror; or a lawyer shall not contact or solicit professional employment either in-person or by live telephone from any person who is not a lawyer, family member, or former client. Model Rules 4.2, 3.5, & 7.3.

The rule to remember is that when communication by a lawyer is banned, it's banned in almost every instance regardless of who contacts whom first. (Except, of course, that the lawyer may discuss a matter with a prospective client who initiates the contact.) Thus, for instance, if a juror tries to strike up a conversation with one of the lawyers in a case, the lawyer has to terminate the conversation immediately. It's quite common on the MPRE for a distracter to suggest that a communication is proper because someone other than the lawyer in the fact pattern initiated the contact. Don't be fooled by this device!

(4) An attorney may not engage in conduct that would cause a judge to violate the Model Code of Judicial Conduct.

Sometimes an MPRE fact pattern will point to a judge who has violated the Model Code of Judicial Conduct with the help of a lawyer. A common example concerns a judge who contacts a lawyer because he or she happens to be an expert on a particular issue in a case, instead of relying solely on the briefs submitted by counsel.

Although there's nothing in the Model Rules that discourages a lawyer from advising a judge on the law, the Model Code of Judicial Conduct itself requires that a judge refrain from relying on the advice unless the judge first tells the lawyers in the case the name of the expert consulted and the substance of his or her advice, and gives the lawyers a chance to respond. Model

Code of Judicial Conduct, Rule 2.9(A)(2). Remember, therefore, that it's not enough to know the Model Rules. When a judge is involved, you have to include the Model Code of Judicial Conduct in your analysis of a lawyer's conduct. Under Model Rule 8.4(f), a lawyer can't knowingly aid a judge in violating the law *or the Model Code of Judicial Conduct.* Thus, if a judge's conduct violates the Model Code of Judicial Conduct and a lawyer has helped the judge in that conduct, the lawyer has violated the ethics rules.

(5) A client's insistence on a course of conduct doesn't relieve the lawyer of the responsibility to observe the Rules.

Sometimes an MPRE fact pattern will feature an attorney who has violated the Rules at the insistence of the client — for example, asserting an unmeritorious or baseless claim for the sake of harassing the adversary, or taking on work when the lawyer isn't competent to handle it. Rule to remember: The client's insistence on improper conduct by the lawyer doesn't relieve the lawyer of the obligation not to engage in the conduct.

c. Traps set by the Examiners

Knowing the tricks the examiners use to lure you into choosing the wrong answer can save you from the temptation to pick them instead of the right answer. When the examiners create an MPRE, their central concern is to preserve the integrity of the exam. They want people who know the Rules to pass the exam, and people who don't know the Rules to fail. (In fact, this is the only way they can convince the states to include the exam as part of their licensing requirements.) So, what they do is to set "traps" for the unwary.

It's almost as though they deliberately calculate and anticipate the mistakes students are likely to make and build around them. They design and construct "distracters" — wrong answers — precisely to lure everyone into making these very mistakes.

(1) The "Hmmm, that sounds familiar" trap

This is the most common — and most insidious — trap on the MPRE. Many law students have a tendency to review for exams only until they can respond by rote. They don't bother to analyze the material to the point of real understanding, and they especially don't bother to apply the material to real facts. The MPRE examiners know this about law students, so they construct answers that seem right because they correctly state a rule or a part of a rule — *EXCEPT THAT* the rule they state is not the rule that applies to the facts. Here's an example:

> An attorney represented a landlord in a variety of matters over several years. An elderly widow living on public assistance filed suit against the landlord alleging that the landlord withheld without justification the security deposit on a rental unit that she had vacated three years ago. She brought the action for herself, without counsel, in small claims court. The attorney investigated the claim and learned that it was legally barred by the applicable statute of limitations, although the widow's underlying claim was meritorious. The attorney told the landlord of the legal defense, but emphasized that the widow's claim was just and that, in all fairness, the security deposit should be returned to the widow. The attorney told the landlord:

>> "I strongly recommend that you pay her the full amount with interest. It is against your long-term business interests to be known in the community as a landlord who routinely withholds security deposits even though the tenant leaves the apartment in good condition. Paying the claim now will prevent future headaches for you."

> Was the attorney's conduct proper?

> **(A)** Yes, if the landlord did not object to the attorney's advice and paid the widow's claim.

> **(B)** Yes, because the attorney may refer to both legal and non-legal considerations in advising a client.

> **(C)** No, unless the attorney's engagement letter informed the landlord that the attorney's advice on the matter would include both legal and non-legal considerations.

> **(D)** No, because in advising the landlord to pay the full claim, the attorney failed to represent zealously the landlord's legal interests.

Look at option D. This is a tempting choice because it sounds familiar; you may even say to yourself, "I've seen something like this in one of the Rules, so it must be right." In fact, that language is contained in Model Rule 1.3, Comment [1]. The problem is that the language used — the responsibility of a lawyer to act with zeal — is not what the facts are getting at. Ultimately, Option D is wrong because it's not directed at whether the attorney's advice, which went beyond purely technical legal advice, was proper, and that's the issue here.

Option C does the same thing, but this time it suggests a different but equally inapplicable Rule. The idea of an engagement letter will ring a bell, but such a letter to the client is concerned with fees. Its purpose is to make clear what services the lawyer will provide and what he or she will charge for them, not in what form he or she will render advice. Model Rule 1.5.

Ultimately, these answer options are tempting because they reference the Rules in a way that is familiar, and unless you realize that the pivotal issue here concerns the appropriate scope of a lawyer's advice to a client, you might choose C or D. Don't think examiners don't realize this when they create answer options like this! (Incidentally, the best response is B. A lawyer should exercise professional judgment and give candid advice, which may rely on considerations other than purely technical legal advice.)

The only way to insulate yourself against this kind of trap is to study and know the Rules. If you are sufficiently familiar with the Rules, you'll be able to distinguish one Rule from another.

(2) Stating part of a rule, and omitting a part that would change the result

A frequent trick in distracters is the partial statement of a Rule, or the statement of a Rule without including a relevant or controlling exception. For example:

> An attorney filed an action on behalf of a client for breach of contract. In fact, the client had no legal basis for the suit, but wanted to harass the defendant. To induce the attorney to file the action, the client made certain false statements of material fact to the attorney, which the attorney included in the complaint filed against the defendant.
>
> At the trial of the case, the client took the stand and testified as set forth in the complaint. The trial court ordered

judgment for the client. After entry of judgment, the client wrote the attorney a letter marked "Confidential," in which the client admitted that she had lied to the attorney and had testified falsely in the case.

Upon complaint of the defendant, who claimed the attorney had knowingly used false testimony in the case, disciplinary proceedings were instituted against the attorney.

Is it proper for the attorney to use the client's letter in the attorney's defense in the disciplinary proceedings?

(A) Yes, if it is necessary to do so in order to protect the attorney's rights.

(B) Yes, because the client had committed a fraud on the court in which the case was tried.

(C) No, because the attorney learned the facts from the client in confidence.

(D) No, if disclosure by the attorney could result in the client's prosecution for perjury.

Look at option C. It suggests the *general* rule prohibiting a lawyer from revealing any information relating to the representation of a client without the client's consent, but it ignores the *exception* to this rule, which is core to these facts. The exception is that a lawyer *may reveal* a client confidence to defend him- or herself in a controversy with the client or against a criminal charge or civil claim for conduct involving the client, or to respond to allegations in any proceeding concerning the representation. Model Rule 1.6(b). Because the exception is the important point here, the correct answer is A. Thus, *whenever* an answer option seems to state a prevailing Rule, be on your guard — don't accept the statement at face value — scan your memory to verify that the Rule has been stated either completely or in *pertinent* part, and pay special attention to all the exceptions you know.

(3) Focusing on an issue that wasn't addressed in the "call" of the question

Sometimes when you read a fact pattern on the MPRE, an issue you've learned well will jump off the page at you. You'll immediately assume that's the issue on which the question is focusing, but don't let yourself be distracted. Focus *only* on what's asked in the *call* of the question. If it's a specific call, and it doesn't elicit the issue that first jumped out at you, you can be sure that one of the distracters will rely on that very issue — and, of course, it's one of the three wrong answers. (Remember, this rule applies only to questions following a *specific* call. If the call of the question is general — for example, "Is the attorney subject to discipline for his conduct?" — then the issue you first spotted may well be the basis for the correct answer.)

d. Modifiers can lead you to the best response

Remember that the basic format for MPRE answer options looks like this: *"No, if the psychiatrist is not compensated in any way for referring cases to the attorney."* The first word, "Yes" or "No," states the *result*. The word immediately after the comma is the *modifier*. The remainder of the answer is the *reasoning behind the result*. Your instinct will tell you that the reasoning is the most important part of the answer option. But frequently that one-word modifier — the "if," "unless," or "because" immediately after the comma — is as important as the reasoning itself! Learning how to analyze answers based on their modifiers will dramatically improve your chances of answering any MPRE question correctly.

The examiners use three kinds of modifiers on the MPRE — "because," "if," and "unless." These are studied in more detail below.

(1) The definite modifier — "because"

"Because" is a *definite,* as opposed to a *conditional,* modifier. Simply put, when "because" is the modifier, it must *necessarily* be true that the reasoning leads to the result. For an answer beginning with "because" to be correct, the following three elements must exist.

(a) Resolve central issue

The reasoning must address and resolve an issue central to the call of the question — or, at least, an issue more central than any other response.

(b) Unequivocally reflect facts

The facts in the reasoning must *completely* and *unequivocally* confirm the facts in the basic fact pattern. For instance, if an option states, "because there was a conflict between two of his clients," the facts must *clearly* show a conflict between the two clients.

(c) Agreement between result and reasoning

The result must be consistent with the reasoning. For instance, if the reasoning tells you, "because the representation was competent," the result must be that the representation is proper. Keep in mind, however, that if the lawyer's competence isn't the central issue, this element *alone* will not necessarily make the option the best response.

Although this is fairly technical, the example below should illustrate this further.

> Four years ago, an attorney was a judge in a state court of general jurisdiction and heard a plaintiff's civil case against a defendant. The plaintiff prevailed and secured a judgment for $50,000, which was sustained on appeal. Since then, the attorney has resigned from the bench and returned to private practice. The defendant has filed suit to enjoin enforcement of the judgment on the grounds of extrinsic fraud in its procurement. The plaintiff has now asked the attorney to represent the plaintiff in defending the suit to enjoin enforcement.

Is it proper for the attorney to accept the representation of the plaintiff in this matter?

(A) Yes, because the attorney would be upholding the decision of the court.

(B) Yes, if the attorney's conduct of the first trial will not be in issue.

(C) No, unless the attorney believes the present suit is brought in bad faith.

(D) No, because the attorney had acted in a judicial capacity on the merits of the original case.

Look at option D, a "because" answer option. By the time you read option D, you should have determined that the *problem* here is the conflict of interest that can arise when a lawyer moves from the judiciary to private practice. The rule is that a lawyer can't represent anyone in connection with a matter in which the lawyer participated personally and substantially as a judge, unless all parties to the proceeding give informed, written consent. Model Rule 1.12(a).

Now, go through the three elements for the "because" modifier to see if D is correct. Remember, the shorthand for those three elements is: (1) resolves a central issue; (2) unequivocally reflects the facts; and (3) shows agreement between result and reasoning.

First, does option D address and resolve a central issue? Yes, it does; the issue is whether the attorney can properly represent the plaintiff, and this turns on whether his conflict of interest prevents him from doing so. D cites the rule on conflicts of interest for former judges, the central issue, so D passes the first hurdle.

The second hurdle is determining whether the reasoning unequivocally reflects the facts. It does. You're told that the attorney was the judge in the original suit, and the new suit deals with the enforceability of that judgment. Thus, as option D indicates, the attorney did in fact participate "personally and substantially" as a judge in the original case.

Finally, the result and the reasoning must agree. Because the reasoning in D is true, then a conflict of interest must exist that would prevent the attorney from representing the plaintiff. Option D tells you that it would not be proper for the attorney to represent the plaintiff under these facts. Thus, the result and the reasoning agree. (Note, incidentally, that representing the plaintiff would not only be improper — it would subject the attorney to discipline; but, then, every disciplinable act or omission is necessarily improper.)

Now that you've seen how you can determine if a "because" option is correct, you can see how you can conclude that some "because" answers are *incorrect*. Look at option A, which also begins with the modifier "because." Look directly at the three "hurdles," the first one first. Does the reasoning of the option address and resolve a central issue? *No*. The central issue is conflict, so it doesn't matter whether the attorney is upholding his decision or not; what matters is that he was acting as judge in the first trial and that this creates an irreconcilable conflict in the second trial. Because option A fails to clear the first hurdle, you can move on to the next option; you've eliminated A as an acceptable response.

If you have difficulty determining whether a "because" option is correct, there is a way that may help you. Combine the reasoning of the answer with the call of the question to create an "if-then" statement. If the "if-then" statement is true, the answer is correct. If you do this with answer A, you wind up with the following statement: "If the attorney is upholding the decision of the court, then it would be proper for the attorney to represent the plaintiff." As you can see, the "if" clause is the reasoning in the original answer, and the "then" statement restates the call of the question. For the statement to be true, the "if" clause must provide a valid reason for the resulting "then" element. In answer A, it doesn't — the fact that the attorney isn't challenging the judgment doesn't resolve the conflict of interest in favor of his representing the plaintiff. If you're stuck on a "because" option, try rewording it in this way to help clarify whether or not it's correct.

Incidentally, did you notice what kind of a "distracter" option A is? It's one in which the reasoning evokes a rule that seems correct but *doesn't apply* to the facts. Option A evokes the lawyer's duty of loyalty to former clients — i.e., the Rule that states a lawyer can't represent a new client with interests adverse to a former client in a substantially related matter. Model Rule 1.9(a). (For instance, a lawyer can't seek to rescind on behalf of a new client a contract he or she drafted for an old client, or challenge the validity of a will for a descendant that he or she prepared and witnessed for the decedent.) Option A suggests that because the attorney isn't challenging his own judgment, his representation of the plaintiff is proper. Of course, this is wrong, because the conflict exists *independently* of whether the attorney is challenging his own decision. Nonetheless, you can see why bringing up another rule makes A a good distracter.

(2) The conditional modifiers: — "if" and "unless"

"If" and "unless" are called conditional responses, because the result is conditional on the reasoning. Such answer options are very common on the MPRE.

When you see "if" or "unless" as a modifier in an answer option, the reasoning will do one of two things:

— It will clarify ambiguous facts in the fact pattern; or

— It will add facts that resolve a central issue.

To better understand how to deal with these responses on the MPRE, you should look at each modifier separately.

(a) When "if" is the modifier

For an "if" option to be the best response, it must overcome these three hurdles:

(1) Plausibility

The reasoning must be *plausible* on the facts — that is, there can't be anything in the facts to suggest the statement *cannot* be true. (Of course, this also means that the reasoning can't be *unequivocally* established by the facts, either.) For example, say the issue in an MPRE question is incompetence, and you're told that an attorney went on a three-month drunken binge and neglected to file his client's complaint before the statute of limitations ran out. If the call of the question asked you whether the attorney was subject to discipline, a response would not be correct if it said, "Yes, *if* he rendered incompetent representation," because the facts show that the attorney's conduct was *unquestionably* incompetent; there's no realistic way to deem the attorney's service competent, so the statement can't be considered plausible.

(2) Central issue

The reasoning must address a *central issue*. For an "if" option to be correct, it must either add essential facts or clarify existing facts in such a way as to resolve a central issue. The easiest way to show what this means is with an example.

The law firm of Alpha and Beta has a radio commercial which states:

"Do you have a legal problem? Are you being sued? Consult Alpha and Beta, licensed attorneys at law. Initial conference charge is $25 for one hour. Act now and protect your interests. Call at 1234 Main Street; telephone area code (101) 123-4567."

Are Alpha and Beta subject to discipline for the commercial?

(A) Yes, because the qualifications of the lawyers are not stated.

(B) Yes, because the radio broadcast may encourage litigation.

(C) No, if all the statements in the radio broadcast are true.

(D) No, unless the radio broadcast is heard outside the state in which they are licensed.

Let's look at option C. Remember the first two hurdles — plausibility and central issue. The first hurdle option C must clear to be the best response is to be *plausible* under the facts. The facts tell you that Alpha and Beta have a radio commercial and give you the content of the commercial. Thus, it's plausible — neither definite nor impossible — that the statements in the commercial are true, so option C clears the first hurdle.

Now you have to see if it clears the second hurdle — namely, does option C address a *central issue* raised by the facts? To do that, you have to step back a minute and call up the Rule that is brought up by these facts. The issue is whether the advertisement is acceptable under Model Rule 7.2, which allows a lawyer to advertise by any public medium or through written or recorded media. Model Rule 7.2 is subject to Model Rule 7.1, however, which requires that the advertisement not be false or misleading.

The facts do not tell you whether the statements in the advertisement are false or misleading, but option C supplies the essential fact that they are not. In doing do, it resolves the central issue.

(3) Agreement between result and reasoning

The result and the reasoning must agree. If you conclude that an "if" option is plausible under the facts and that it resolves a central issue in the facts, it still has one last hurdle to clear: the result — before the comma introducing "if" — and the reasoning — after the comma following "if" — must agree. In the sample problem, if the statements are true, Alpha and Beta will not be subject to discipline. Because the call of the question asks you if they'll be subject to discipline, the result would have to be "no." Since it is, option C must be the best response — and it is.

Note that if the reasoning stated the opposite fact, the result would also have to state the opposite for option C to be correct. That is, if the reasoning were "The statements weren't true," then the result would have to be "yes" in order for the option to be correct. So if you reversed both the result and the reasoning in option C, it would say, "Yes, if the statements were false." Incidentally, note that in this reverse form option C *still* would be correct because it would be plausible under the facts, it would resolve a central issue, and its result and reasoning would agree.

(b) When "unless" is the modifier

Like "if," "unless" is a conditional modifier. In fact, "if" and "unless" are *almost* mirror images of each other. (But note one difference between them — a correct "if" response provides circumstances under which the result might occur; when "unless" is the modifier, the *reasoning must provide the only circumstance under which the result would not occur* before the option can be the best response.) For instance, if the call of the question asks you whether an attorney's conduct is proper, and an answer option begins "No, unless," the reasoning must provide the only way that would make the attorney's conduct proper. If instead, the call of the question asks you whether an attorney is subject to discipline, and an answer option begins, "Yes, unless," the reasoning of that option must supply the only way that enables an attorney to *avoid* discipline. If you can think of even *one other way* in which the same result could occur, an option containing "unless" *cannot* be the best response.

As with "if" answers, the reasoning in a correct "unless" response will either clarify the facts in the fact pattern, or provide an additional fact that resolves a central issue. For example:

> An attorney was retained by a client to incorporate the client's business, which previously had been operated as a sole proprietorship. The attorney noticed in the client's file copies of some correspondence from the client to another attorney concerning the possibility of the other attorney incorporating the client's business. The attorney questioned the client to make certain that any attorney-client relationship between the other attorney and the client had been terminated. The client told the attorney,
>
> > "It certainly has been terminated. When I discussed the matter with that guy six months ago, he asked for a retainer of $1,000, which I paid him. He did absolutely nothing after he got the money, even though I called him weekly, and finally, last week when I again complained, he returned the retainer. But don't say anything about it because he is an old friend of my family."

Is the attorney subject to discipline if she does not report her knowledge of the other attorney's conduct to the appropriate authority?

(A) Yes, if the attorney believes the other attorney clearly was guilty of professional misconduct.

(B) Yes, unless the attorney believes the other attorney does not usually neglect matters entrusted to him.

(C) No, if the client was satisfied by the other attorney's return of the retainer.

(D) No, unless the client agrees that the attorney may report the information.

Look at option D. When you read the call of this question, you should have recognized that the issue was whether or not the attorney was required to report the other attorney's misconduct. You should also have summoned to mind the rule on a lawyer's duty to report another lawyer's violation of the Model Rules of Professional Conduct if the violation raises a substantial question as to that lawyer's honesty, trustworthiness, or fitness as a lawyer. Model Rule 8.3(a). However, when information about the violation is protected under the confidentiality rules of Model Rule 1.6, the duty becomes discretionary rather than absolute. If the client whose confidentiality would be breached does not give consent to the disclosure, a lawyer need not report the violation.

Ultimately, Option D provides the only situation where the attorney would not be subject to discipline if she does not report the other attorney's conduct to the appropriate authority.

Remember, "unless" and "if" are *almost* mirror images. If you change option D a little bit, you can see how this works. Say option D, instead of "No, unless . . ." said "Yes, if the client has agreed that the attorney may report the information." Note that the reasoning is plausible, it addresses and resolves a central issue, and the reasoning and the result agree. Thus, "if" makes option D correct in the same way as "unless."

Keep in mind, however, that "if" and "unless" aren't perfect mirror images, because "unless" requires exclusivity, and "if" doesn't. Looking at option D with "if" as the modifier, you can see that it's offering one way in which the attorney's conduct would be made proper — getting the client's consent — but it doesn't exclude other ways. On the other hand, when "No, unless . . ." begins the option, the reasoning that follows states the only way in which the result could occur; in other words, it states the only way for the attorney to avoid discipline on these facts. A perfect mirror image of "unless," then, would not be "if" alone, but "if and only if."

This whole discourse on modifiers and exactly what they mean may strike you as overly technical when applied to such simple words as "if" and "unless." Be assured, however, if you're thoroughly familiar with this method for analyzing modifiers, you'll be well on your way to avoiding the wrong answers.

E. Finding the Right Answer

Learning how to analyze answers correctly can do more for you than simply help you avoid pitfalls. If you put to work all of the principles discussed here, you'll frequently be able to pick the right answer to an MPRE question on first reading! Of course, you shouldn't rush to judgment, because the MPRE is an important exam; the point is that you can learn to increase your confidence and trust your instincts. Your ability to do this is built on something mentioned earlier — namely, the tension between the flexibility inherent in the ethics rules and the need for concrete answers to standardized multiple-choice questions. As a result of this tension, the answer options often contain so many qualifying facts that they lead you directly to the one best choice. For example, here are the four answer options to a past MPRE question:

(A) Yes, unless the attorney's time was completely occupied with work for other clients.

(B) Yes, because the attorney neglected the representation of the passenger.

(C) No, because the passenger's suit was filed before the statute of limitations ran.

(D) No, because the attorney returned the $1,000 retainer to the passenger.

Without first having read the corresponding fact pattern, you should be able to guess the best response. A quick glance at each of the options should tell you that the facts probably revolve around a lawyer who didn't act promptly enough in representing his or her client. Remember, good distracters often focus on the same issue as the best response does. This should suggest to you that the issue raised by the fact pattern requires an analysis of the standard set by Mode Rule 1.3 to determine whether a lawyer has acted diligently and promptly in representing the client. You know that the rule requires a lawyer to act with "reasonable diligence and promptness." You also know that a lawyer should control his or her workload to avoid neglecting one client in favor of others and that unreasonable delay is unacceptable even if the client's interests are not affected in substance. That makes it easy to eliminate options A and C. Option D cannot be the right answer because the issue is neglect of the passenger's interests, not the retainer. With all of that in mind, the best answer is almost certainly option B.

To prove the validity of this approach, here are the facts to this same question:

> An attorney was retained by a passenger on a bus who had been injured in a collision between the bus and a truck. The passenger paid the attorney a retainer of $1,000 and agreed further that the attorney should have a fee of 25 percent of any recovery before filing suit, 30 percent of any recovery after suit was filed but before judgment, and 35 percent of any recovery after trial and judgment. The attorney promptly called the lawyer for the bus company and told him she was representing the passenger and would like to talk about a settlement. The attorney made an appointment to talk to the lawyer for the bus company, but did not keep the appointment. The attorney continued to put off talking to the lawyer for the bus company. Meanwhile, the passenger became concerned because she had heard nothing from the attorney. The passenger called the attorney's office but was told the attorney was not in and would not call back. The passenger was told not to worry because the attorney would look after her interests. After 10 months had passed, the passenger went to another attorney for advice. The other attorney advised the passenger that the statute of limitations would run in one week and, with the passenger's consent, immediately filed suit for the passenger. The attorney, upon the passenger's demand, refunded the $1,000 the passenger had paid.
>
> Is the attorney subject to discipline?

As you can see, the facts confirm that B is the best response. This should give you the confidence to trust your instincts as you measure the answer options under facts such as these. Here is another example of four answer options.

(A) Yes, because the attorney has no interest in the case.

(B) Yes, if the judge believes that the attorney's advice is needed to serve the interests of justice.

(C) No, unless all parties in the case first give their written consent to the judge's consultation with the attorney.

(D) No, unless the judge informs the parties of the attorney's identity and the substance of the attorney's advice, and asks for their responses.

Try to deduce what facts are behind these options. You can logically assume that the judge has consulted the attorney (who is probably not an attorney for one of the parties — option A tells us that he has no interest in the case). That's implied by all of the answer options, and, as you know by now, distracters are only effective if they contain elements common to the correct answer. Consequently, it seems Model Code of Judicial Conduct Rule 2.9(A)(2) is at issue here. It permits a judge to consult a disinterested party on applicable law providing he or she follows certain guidelines. The answer options should tell you that the fact pattern probably concerns a judge who asked an uninterested party for advice concerning a proceeding before him or her and that option D is probably the best answer. Here are the facts from that question:

A judge is presiding in a case that has, as its main issue, a complicated point of commercial law. The lawyers have not presented the case to the judge's satisfaction, and the judge believes she needs additional legal advice. The judge's former partner in law practice is an attorney and expert in the field of law that is at issue. The attorney has no interest in the case.

Is it proper for the judge to consult the attorney?

As you can see, reading the facts, as in the last example, only reinforces your judgment that the best answer is option D. Here is one more set of options:

(A) Yes, because the client instructed the attorney not to tell anyone about the jewelry box.

(B) Yes, if the disclosure would be detrimental to the client's interests.

(C) No, because the jewelry box was not involved in the dispute between the client and his partner.

(D) No, if the disclosure is necessary to enable the attorney to defend against a criminal charge.

Looking at these options, you can reasonably assume that the facts revolve around confidentiality. A lawyer has a duty not to reveal information relating to the representation of a client without the client's consent. Model Rule 1.6(a). An exception to the rule, however, is the lawyer's right to defend himself or herself against a criminal charge based on conduct in which the client was involved. Model Rule 1.6(b)(5). Because option D clearly outlines this exception to the client-confidentiality rule, it is very likely the best answer.

The facts to this question bear this out:

An attorney had been representing the client for several months in a matter involving the ownership of some antique jewelry. The client claimed he purchased the jewelry for his wife with his own funds. The client's business partner claimed the jewelry was a partnership purchase in which he had a one-half interest. While the matter was pending, the client brought a valuable antique jewelry box to the attorney's office and said:

"Keep this in your vault for me. I bought it before I went into business with my partner. Do not tell him or anyone else about it until my matter with my partner is settled."

Later that same day, a police officer, who was in the attorney's office on another matter, saw the jewelry box when a clerk opened the vault to put in some papers. The police officer recognized it as one that had recently been stolen from a collector. The attorney was arrested and later charged with receiving stolen property.

Is the attorney subject to discipline if the attorney reveals that the client brought the box to her office?

If you are sufficiently well-versed in analyzing answer options to MPRE questions and relating them to the facts, you'll be so well prepared for the MPRE that you could well pass the exam just by reasoning your way through the options without reading the questions! But don't get the wrong idea. In no way should you skip the facts.

On the contrary, you should read and reread every fact pattern before you consider the options. And then trust the skills and the instinct you've developed by reviewing and understanding the rules, studying this book, and reasoning your way to the right answers.

Good luck.

Part Two
Model Questions and Answers

Part Two contains 60 questions reproduced from **MPRE Sample Questions VI and MPRE Online Practice Exam 1**, published by the National Conference of Bar Examiners. With these model questions, you should be able to put into practice the plan of attack you learned in Part One. The 60 model questions are followed by an explanation and analysis of the answer options. The answers begin on page 86 and reflect the Model Rules of Professional Conduct and the Model Code of Judicial Conduct.

A couple of brief words of advice before you get started. First of all, don't pay attention to timing as you read. On the real MPRE, you'll have two minutes for each question. But for now, put that out of your mind. When you practice here, it's much more important to pay attention to applying the principles from Part One than to beat the clock. Speed will come naturally as you become more proficient at reading the questions and choosing among the answers. Save working on speed until you do the questions in Part Three.

Also, if you pick the wrong answer option, don't stop after you read the correct response; read why the option you chose is wrong. (It's a good idea to make a study sheet of these "near misses" as you answer the questions — see more on what to do with this sheet in Part Three). Each response is designed to show you not only the correct Rule, but, far more importantly, the mistake you made when you chose the wrong response. You may actually learn more from analyzing the wrong answer than from reviewing the right answer!

In terms of breaking up the questions, you'd be wise to do ten or so model questions, check your results, and then proceed. Breaking your review down into small chunks like this, and reviewing answers as you go, gives you a chance to identify and correct any mistakes you make before they become habits. If you feel very confident from the start, though, there's no reason why you can't just do all 60 questions at once and then review the answers.

A. Model Questions

Question 1.

An attorney practices in a state that does not require lawyers to participate in continuing legal education courses. After the attorney forms a partnership with several other lawyers, the majority decides that the firm will not pay for continuing legal education courses since they are not required by the state. Consequently, the attorney tells the firm he will not attend any continuing legal education courses.

Is it proper for the attorney to refuse to attend any continuing legal education courses?

(A) Yes, unless the state offers free continuing legal education courses.

(B) Yes, if the attorney independently undertakes continuing study and education in the law.

(C) No, because the attorney cannot maintain competence without attending continuing legal education courses.

(D) No, unless the attorney obtains malpractice insurance.

Question 2.

An attorney is a newly admitted member of the bar. A partner in his firm was recognized as an expert in securities regulation law. A corporation retained the firm to qualify the corporation's stock for public sale. After accepting the matter, the partner preferred to spend his time on cases with larger fee potential, so he assigned the corporation matter to the attorney. The attorney told the partner he knew nothing about securities regulation law and that he had too little time to prepare himself for the corporation's sale without substantial help from the partner. The partner refused to help and directed the attorney to proceed.

Was the partner's conduct proper in this matter?

(A) Yes, because as a member of the bar, the attorney is licensed to handle any legal matter.

(B) Yes, because the partner may withdraw from a case if work on it would cause him unreasonable financial hardship.

(C) No, because the partner knew the attorney was not competent to handle the matter, and the partner failed to provide supervision adequate to protect the client's interest.

:49

(D) No, because the corporation had not given the partner permission to assign the attorney to work on the matter.

Question 3.

An attorney is a member of the bar in State First and is also licensed as a stockbroker in State Second. In his application for renewal of his stockbroker's license in State Second, the attorney knowingly filed a false financial statement.

:19

Is the attorney subject to discipline in State First?

(A) Yes, because his actions involve dishonesty or misrepresentation.

(B) Yes, but only if he is first convicted of a criminal offense in State Second.

(C) No, because his action was not done in his capacity as an attorney.

(D) No, because his action was not in State First.

Question 4.

An attorney is a sole practitioner whose practice is largely in the areas of tax, wills, estates, and trusts. The attorney learned of a new Internal Revenue Service (IRS) regulation that probably affects the trust provisions in a will she prepared for a client two years ago. The attorney has not represented the client since she drew up the will.

Is the attorney subject to discipline if she calls the former client and advises her of the new IRS ruling and the need to revise the will?

:39

(A) Yes, if the attorney has any reason to believe that the former client has another lawyer.

(B) Yes, because the attorney would be soliciting legal business from a person who is not a current client.

(C) No, provided the attorney does not thereafter prepare a new will for the former client.

(D) No, because the client is a former client of the attorney.

Question 5.

An attorney was retained to appeal the client's criminal conviction and to seek bail pending appeal. The agreed fee for the appearance on the bail hearing was $50 per hour. The attorney received $800 from the client, of which $300 was a deposit to secure the attorney's fee, and $500 was for bail costs in the event that bail was obtained. The attorney maintained two office bank accounts: a "Fee Account," in which all fees were deposited and from which all office expenses were paid, and a "Clients' Fund Account." The attorney deposited the $800 in the "Clients' Fund Account" the week before the bail hearing. The attorney expended six hours of time on the bail hearing. The effort to obtain bail was unsuccessful. Dissatisfied, the client immediately demanded return of the $800.

It is now proper for the attorney to:

(A) transfer the $800 to the "Fee Account"?

(B) transfer $300 to the "Fee Account" and leave $500 in the "Clients' Fund Account" until the attorney's fee for the final appeal is determined?

(C) transfer $300 to the "Fee Account" and send the client a $500 check on the "Clients' Fund Account"?

(D) send the client a $500 check and leave $300 in the "Clients' Fund Account" until the matter is resolved?

Question 6.

A judge has been assigned to try a criminal prosecution by the state against a defendant. Ten years previously, the judge, while serving as a deputy attorney general in the state, initiated an investigation of the defendant for suspected criminal conduct. The investigation did not establish any basis for prosecution. None of the matters previously investigated is involved in or affects the present prosecution.

Is it proper for the judge to try the case?

(A) Yes, because none of the matters previously investigated is involved in or affects the present case.

(B) Yes, unless the judge might be prejudiced against the defendant because of the prior investigation.

(C) No, if the judge had substantial responsibility in initiating the previous investigation of defendant.

(D) No, if the judge had substantial responsibility in determining that the previous investigation did not establish any basis for prosecution.

Question 7.

An attorney represented a landlord in a variety of matters over several years. An elderly widow living on public assistance filed suit against the landlord alleging that the landlord withheld without justification the security deposit on a rental unit that the widow vacated three years ago. She brought the action for herself, without counsel, in small claims court. The attorney investigated the claim and learned that it was legally barred by the applicable statute of limitations, although the widow's underlying claim was meritorious. The attorney told the landlord of the legal defense, but emphasized that the widow's claim was just and that, in all fairness, the security deposit should be returned to her. The attorney told the landlord:

> "I strongly recommend that you pay the widow the full amount with interest. It is against your long-term business interests to be known in the community as a landlord who routinely withholds security deposits even though the tenant leaves the apartment in good condition. Paying the claim now will prevent future headaches for you."

Was the attorney's conduct proper?

1:04

(A) Yes, if the landlord did not object to the attorney's advice and paid the widow's claim.

(B) Yes, because the attorney may refer to both legal and non-legal considerations in advising a client.

(C) No, unless the attorney's engagement letter informed the landlord that the attorney's advice on the matter would include both legal and non-legal considerations.

(D) No, because in advising the landlord to pay the full claim, the attorney failed to represent zealously the landlord's legal interests.

Question 8.

An attorney is a member of the bar and a salaried employee of a bank's trust department. As part of his duties, he prepares a monthly newsletter concerning wills, trusts, estates, and taxes, which the bank sends to all of its customers. The newsletter contains a recommendation to the customer to review his or her will in light of the information contained and, if the customer has any questions, to bring the will to the bank, where the attorney will review the customer's will and answer the customer's legal questions. The bank provides the attorney's services to its customers for no charge.

Is the attorney subject to discipline for the foregoing?

(A) Yes, because by sending out the newsletter the attorney is giving legal advice to persons who are not his clients.

(B) Yes, because the attorney is assisting the bank in the unauthorized practice of law.

(C) No, because no charge is made for the attorney's advice.

(D) No, because the attorney is a member of the bar.

Question 9.

An attorney was recently admitted to practice and was hired as a new associate at a large firm employing over 100 lawyers. The attorney was working late one night when he received a telephone call from his cousin. His cousin said that he was calling from the police station where he had just been arrested for possession of cocaine with intent to distribute. He was permitted to make only one phone call, and the attorney was the only lawyer he knew. The attorney responded that he had no criminal law experience and that his firm did not handle criminal cases. Nevertheless, his cousin pleaded with the attorney to come to the police station and see what he could do to get him out on bail. The attorney replied that he would do what he could.

The attorney went to the police station and using what information he recalled from his criminal law and procedure courses attempted to get his cousin released on bail. However, as a result of his inexperience, the attorney was unable to secure his cousin's release that night. The next morning, the attorney found an experienced criminal lawyer for his cousin, who obtained his cousin's release within one hour.

Was the attorney's conduct proper?

(A) Yes, because neither referral nor consultation was practical under the circumstances.

(B) Yes, because the attorney was a close relative.

(C) No, because the attorney had no special training or experience in criminal cases.

(D) No, because the attorney did not have the requisite level of competence to accept representation in the case.

Question 10.

A business attorney entered into a partnership with a certified public accountant. The partnership provided legal and other assistance to clients in connection with business and tax planning, tax filings, and other personal and corporate business matters. The accountant performed only work that she was authorized to perform as a certified public accountant. The attorney made reasonable efforts to ensure that the accountant did not interfere with the attorney's compliance with his professional obligations as a lawyer.

Is the attorney subject to discipline?

(A) Yes, because some of the activities of the partnership consisted of the practice of law.

(B) Yes, because lawyers may not form partnerships with non-lawyers.

(C) No, because the accountant performed only work that she was authorized to perform as a certified public accountant.

(D) No, because the attorney made reasonable efforts to ensure that the accountant did not interfere with the attorney's compliance with his professional obligations as a lawyer.

Question 11.

An attorney is widely regarded as an exceptionally competent practitioner in the field of criminal law. A client of the attorney became the subject of a grand jury investigation in a matter that could result in a felony indictment. The client lacked sufficient funds to pay for the attorney's services beyond the grand jury stage. He asked the attorney to provide limited representation for a flat fee. Under the arrangement he proposed, the attorney would advise the client concerning the grand jury investigation, but the representation would end when an indictment was returned or the grand jury decided not to indict. The attorney fully advised the client of the practical and legal aspects of the client's proposal.

Is it proper for the attorney to accept this limited representation?

(A) Yes, because the client and not the attorney suggested the arrangement.

(B) Yes, because the attorney and the client may agree to limit the scope of the representation so long as the limitation is reasonable under the circumstances.

(C) No, because the attorney should not limit the scope of the representation based on the client's ability to pay.

(D) No, because the scope of the representation may not be limited in a criminal case.

Question 12.

An attorney represents a client who is under indictment for homicide. In the course of the representation, the client told the attorney that she had previously killed two other people. These murders are completely unrelated to the murder indictment for which the attorney is providing representation. With the client's consent, the attorney made a tape recording of the client's confession regarding the unrelated homicides. At the attorney's request, the client also drew a map of the remote locations of the victims' graves from the unrelated killings. Those bodies have not been found by the police, and the client is not a suspect in either crime, both of which remain unsolved.

Is the attorney subject to discipline if he fails to voluntarily disclose to the authorities his knowledge of the two prior murders and the locations of the victim's bodies?

(A) Yes, because as an officer of the court, the attorney must disclose any knowledge that he has, whether privileged or not, concerning the commission of the prior crimes by his client.

(B) Yes, because the attorney is impeding the state's access to significant evidence.

(C) No, because the attorney did not represent or advise his client with respect to the prior crimes.

(D) No, because the information was obtained by the attorney in the course of the representation.

Question 13.

A client has asked an attorney to represent her in obtaining compensation for a tract of land that is being condemned by the state department of transportation to build a new highway. Two years ago, the attorney had been employed by the department and had been assigned to search title on several tracts of land, including the one owned by the client. The attorney remembers a department engineer had drafted a confidential memorandum advising against running a new highway across the client's land because of a potential adverse environmental impact. Because of this information, the attorney believes it is possible to prevent the condemnation of the client's land or to increase the settlement amount.

What is the proper action for the attorney to take?

1:26

(A) Represent the client on the issue of damages only and not disclose the information that might prevent the condemnation.

(B) Represent the client and attempt to prevent the condemnation by using the information about the adverse environmental impact.

(C) Refuse to represent the client but disclose to her the information about the adverse environmental impact.

(D) Refuse to represent the client and not disclose the information about the adverse environmental impact.

Question 14.

An assistant district attorney was in charge of the presentation before a grand jury of evidence that led to an indictment charging 32 defendants with conspiracy to sell controlled drugs. Shortly after the grand jury returned the indictments, the attorney resigned as assistant district attorney and became an associate in the law office of an attorney for one of the indicted co-defendants.

1:16

Is it proper for that attorney to continue to represent the co-defendant?

(A) Yes, if the former assistant district attorney does not reveal to the attorney any confidence or secret learned while an assistant district attorney.

(B) Yes, because a public prosecutor must make timely disclosure to the defense attorney of any exculpatory evidence.

(C) No, unless the former assistant district attorney agrees not to participate in the representation of the co-defendant.

(D) No, because the former assistant district attorney had substantial responsibility for the indictment of the co-defendant.

Question 15.

An attorney filed an action on behalf of his client for breach of contract. In fact, the client had no legal basis for suit, but wanted to harass the defendant. In order to induce the attorney to file the action, the client made certain false statements of material fact to the attorney, which the attorney included in the complaint filed against the defendant.

At the trial of the case, the client took the stand and testified as set forth in the complaint. The trial court ordered judgment for the client. After entry of judgment, the client wrote the attorney a letter marked "Confidential," in which the client admitted that she had lied to the attorney and had testified falsely in the case.

Upon complaint of the defendant, who claimed the attorney had knowingly used false testimony in the case, disciplinary proceedings were instituted against the attorney.

Is it proper for the attorney to use the client's letter in the attorney's defense in the disciplinary proceedings?

(A) Yes, if it is necessary to do so in order to protect the attorney's rights.

(B) Yes, because the client had committed a fraud on the court in which the case was tried.

(C) No, because the attorney learned the facts from the client in confidence.

(D) No, if disclosure by the attorney could result in the client's prosecution for perjury.

Question 16.

An attorney who is a sole practitioner limits his practice to personal injury cases. He regularly places advertisements in local newspapers that state that his practice is limited to personal injury cases, including medical malpractice. After seeing one of the attorney's ads, a man approached the attorney for representation in a medical malpractice case. After a 30-minute interview, the attorney told the man that he was too busy to take his case because it appeared quite complicated. He further offered to refer the man to another lawyer who regularly practiced in the field. He reminded the man that he should see another lawyer promptly before the statute of limitations expired and he lost his right to sue.

Although the attorney did not charge the man for the interview, the man was upset at wasting 30 minutes of his time. The man did not contact another lawyer until eight months later, when he learned that the statute of limitations on his claim had expired six months after his interview with the attorney. In fact, the man had a meritorious medical malpractice claim.

Is the attorney subject to civil liability?

(A) Yes, because the attorney falsely advertised his availability for medical malpractice cases.

(B) Yes, because the attorney did not advise the man as to the date the statute of limitations would expire.

(C) No, because the attorney did not violate any duty owed to the man.

(D) No, because the attorney offered to refer the man to another medical malpractice lawyer.

Question 17.

An attorney is employed by a client who is a fugitive from justice under indictment for armed robbery. The attorney, after thorough legal research and investigation of the facts furnished by the client, reasonably believes the indictment is fatally defective and should be dismissed as a matter of law. The attorney advised the client of his opinion and urged the client to surrender. The client told the attorney that she would not surrender.

The attorney informed the district attorney that he represented the client and that he had counseled her to surrender but that she refused to follow his advice. The attorney has not advised his client on how to avoid arrest and prosecution and does not know where she is hiding.

Is the attorney subject to discipline if he continues to represent the client?

(A) Yes, because the client is engaging in continuing illegal conduct.

(B) Yes, because the client refused to accept the attorney's advice and surrender.

(C) No, because the attorney is not counseling the client to avoid arrest and prosecution.

(D) No, because the attorney reasonably believes the indictment is defective.

Question 18.

An attorney represented a real estate developer who was trying to buy several properties. The attorney arranged a meeting with an owner of two large parcels of land, hoping to arrange a sale to the developer. When the attorney scheduled this meeting, he neither knew nor asked whether the owner was represented by counsel in the matter. Shortly after the meeting began, the owner disclosed that he had retained counsel to assist in the sale of the two parcels of land, but that his lawyer could not be present that day. He further stated that he would be meeting with his lawyer the next day. The attorney asked the owner if they could talk anyway, and stated that he wouldn't ask the owner to sign anything until his lawyer had a chance to look over anything they discussed.

The owner, an experienced businessman and negotiator, agreed to continue as suggested, and a tentative agreement was soon worked out.

Was the attorney's conduct proper?

(A) Yes, because the owner knowingly agreed to continue the discussions without his own lawyer being present.

(B) Yes, because the attorney did not present the owner with any documents to sign during the meeting.

(C) No, because the attorney negotiated with the owner after learning that the owner was represented by a lawyer in the matter.

(D) No, because the attorney failed to ascertain whether the owner was represented by a lawyer before beginning the negotiation session.

Question 19.

An attorney prepared a will for a client and acted as one of the subscribing witnesses to the client's execution of the will. The will left all of the client's estate to his son. Later, at the client's request, the attorney prepared a second will for the client and acted as one of the subscribing witnesses to the client's execution of the second will. The second will left one-half of the client's estate to his son and the other one-half to his housekeeper. The client died and the housekeeper has offered the second will for probate.

If the son requests that the attorney represent him in opposing probate of the second will on the grounds of fraud and undue influence, is it proper for the attorney to do so?

(A) Yes, because after the client's death the attorney may represent his son.

(B) Yes, because the client's son is a beneficiary under both wills.

(C) No, because an attorney guarantees the validity of a will that he or she prepares.

(D) No, because the attorney would be taking a position adverse to a will she prepared and witnessed.

:51

Question 20.

A judge was trying a case without a jury. After both parties had completed the presentation of evidence and arguments, the judge took the case under advisement.

After the case was under advisement for several weeks, the attorney heard rumors that the judge was having difficulty determining the issue of factual causation and was uncertain about the applicable law. Immediately after hearing these rumors, the attorney telephoned the judge, told the judge of the rumors the attorney had heard, and asked if the judge would like to reopen the case for additional evidence and briefing from both parties. Thereafter, the judge reopened the case for further testimony and requested supplementary briefs from both parties.

Was it proper for the attorney to communicate with the judge?

:54

(A) Yes, because both parties were given full opportunity to present their views on the issues in the case.

(B) Yes, because the attorney did not make any suggestion as to how the judge should decide the matter.

(C) No, because the attorney communicated with the judge on a pending matter without advising opposing counsel.

(D) No, because the attorney caused the judge to reopen a case that had been taken under advisement.

Question 21.

An attorney represented a seller in negotiating the sale of his ice cream parlor. The seller told the attorney in confidence that, although the business had once been very profitable, recent profits had been stable but modest. As the negotiations proceeded, the buyer appeared to be losing interest in the deal. Hoping to restore the buyer's interest, the attorney stated, "The ice cream business is every American's dream: happy kids, steady profits, and a clear conscience." The buyer bought the ice cream parlor but was disappointed when his own profits proved to be modest.

Is the attorney subject to discipline?

(A) Yes, because the attorney made a false statement of fact to the buyer.

(B) Yes, because the attorney exaggerated the profitability of the business.

(C) No, because the attorney represented the seller, not the buyer.

(D) No, because the attorney's statement constitutes acceptable puffing in negotiations.

Question 22.

An attorney has a radio commercial that states:

"Do you have a legal problem? Are you being sued? Call me, a licensed attorney at law. Initial conference charge is $25 for one hour. Act now and protect your interests. Call at 1234 Main Street; telephone area code (101) 123-4567."

Is the attorney subject to discipline for the commercial?

(A) Yes, because the attorney's qualifications are not stated.

(B) Yes, because the radio broadcast may encourage litigation.

(C) No, if all the statements in the radio broadcast are true.

(D) No, unless the radio broadcast is heard outside the state in which the attorney is licensed.

Question 23.

An attorney, recently admitted to practice, opened an office near a residential neighborhood and published the following advertisement in the local newspaper.

COUPON

Get Acquainted With

Your Neighborhood Lawyer

A. Attorney

Suite 2 — 1100 Magnolia Avenue

Sunshine City, State 01000

Telephone: (555) 555-5555

In order to acquaint you with our services, we are offering a one-hour consultation to review your estate plans, including your wills, trusts, and similar documents, all at the nominal cost of $25 to anyone presenting this coupon. Call now for an appointment.

Is the attorney subject to discipline?

(A) Yes, because the attorney is soliciting business from persons with whom the attorney had no prior relationship.

(B) Yes, because the attorney requires the use of a coupon.

(C) No, if the attorney provides the services described for the fee stated.

(D) No, unless the attorney is seeking business from persons who are already represented by a lawyer.

Question 24.

An attorney was retained by a client to incorporate client's business, which previously had been operated as a sole proprietorship. The attorney noticed in the client's file copies of some correspondence from the client to another attorney concerning the possibility of that attorney incorporating the client's business. The attorney questioned the client to make certain that any attorney-client relationship between the other attorney and the client had been terminated. The client told the attorney,

"It certainly has been terminated. When I discussed the matter with that guy six months ago, he asked for a retainer of $1,000, which I paid him. He did absolutely nothing after he got the money, even though I called him weekly, and finally, last week when I again complained, he returned the retainer. But don't say anything about it because he is an old friend of my family."

Is the attorney subject to discipline if she does not report her knowledge of the other attorney's conduct to the appropriate authority?

(A) Yes, if the attorney believes the other attorney was clearly guilty of professional misconduct.

(B) Yes, unless the attorney believes the other attorney does not usually neglect matters entrusted to him.

(C) No, if the client was satisfied by the other attorney's return of the retainer.

(D) No, unless the client agrees that the attorney may report the information.

Question 25.

An attorney represented a client as a plaintiff in a personal injury matter under a standard contingent fee contract. The client agreed to settle the case for $1,000,000, from which funds the attorney would receive $250,000. The client informed the attorney that she planned to take $25,000 of the settlement funds and spend the money purchasing lottery tickets. The attorney told the client that he disagreed with this plan and encouraged the client to take some classes on investing money. The client agreed to take the classes, but still insisted on playing the lottery.

The attorney received the check for $1,000,000 three days before the client was to attend the investing classes. The attorney held the check for one week, giving the client at least a few days of classes. The attorney then informed the client of the receipt of the funds, disbursed the funds according to the agreement, and also furnished the client with an accounting. The attorney told the client that he had delayed notice to allow time for the client to come to her senses. The client laughed and said, "I guess your plan worked, because these classes have convinced me to invest my money in the stock market instead of playing the lottery."

Is the attorney subject to discipline?

(A) Yes, because the attorney had a duty to promptly notify the client of the receipt of the $1,000,000.

(B) Yes, because the attorney gave unsolicited advice about non-legal matters.

(C) No, because the client did not object to the withholding of the notice and funds.

(D) No, because the attorney acted in the client's best interest.

Question 26.

An attorney served two four-year terms as the state's governor immediately prior to reopening his law office in the state. The attorney printed and mailed an announcement of his return to private practice to members of the bar, previous clients, and personal friends whom he had never represented. The printed announcement stated that the attorney had reopened his law office, gave his address and telephone number, and added that he had been the state's governor for the past eight years.

Is the attorney subject to discipline for the announcement?

(A) Yes, because the mailing included persons who had not been his clients.

(B) Yes, because his service as governor is unrelated to his ability as a lawyer.

(C) No, because the information in the announcement was true.

(D) No, because all of the information was already in the public domain.

Question 27.

An attorney has tried many contested cases before a certain judge. The attorney believes the judge is lacking both in knowledge of the law and in good judgment and that another attorney would make an excellent judge. The attorney wishes to help defeat the judge and assist the other attorney in getting elected.

The attorney intends to contribute $5,000 to other attorney's campaign. Is it proper for the attorney to do so?

(A) Yes, the attorney may give $5,000 to the other attorney personally for his campaign.

(B) Yes, if the attorney's contribution to the other attorney is made anonymously.

(C) No, because the attorney is practicing before the court to which the other attorney seeks election.

(D) No, unless the attorney gives the $5,000 to a committee formed to further the other attorney's election.

Question 28.

An attorney practices law in the same community as a lawyer who is running for election as a state judge. The attorney has frequently observed the judicial candidate's courtroom demeanor in litigated cases. Based on those experiences, the attorney believes that the judicial candidate does not have a proper judicial temperament. A local news reporter asked the attorney how he would rate the candidate, and the attorney responded in good faith that he believed the candidate was unsuited for the bench and lacked the proper judicial temperament for a judge. A local newspaper with a wide circulation quoted the attorney's remarks.

Were the attorney's remarks proper?

(A) Yes, because the attorney was not seeking judicial office.

(B) Yes, because the attorney believed the candidate was unsuited for the bench.

(C) No, because the remarks serve to bring the judiciary into disrepute.

(D) No, because a lawyer should not publicly comment on candidates for judicial office.

Question 29.

An attorney was retained by a passenger on a bus who was injured in a collision between the bus and a truck. The passenger paid the attorney a retainer of $1,000, and agreed further that the attorney should have a fee of 25 percent of any recovery before filing suit, 30 percent of any recovery after suit was filed but before judgment, and 35 percent of any recovery after trial and judgment. The attorney promptly called the lawyer for the bus company and told him she was representing the passenger and would like to talk about a settlement. The attorney made an appointment to talk to the lawyer for the bus company, but did not keep the appointment. The attorney continued to put off talking to the lawyer for the bus company. Meanwhile, the passenger became concerned because she had heard nothing from her attorney. The passenger called the attorney's office, but was told the attorney was not in and would not call back. The passenger was told not to worry because the attorney would look after her interests. After ten months had passed, the passenger went to another attorney for advice. The other attorney advised the passenger that the statute of limitations would run in one week and, with the passenger's consent, immediately filed suit for the passenger. Upon the passenger's demand, the attorney refunded the $1,000 the passenger had paid.

Is the attorney subject to discipline?

(A) Yes, unless the attorney's time was completely occupied with work for other clients.

(B) Yes, because the attorney neglected the representation of the passenger.

(C) No, because the passenger's suit was filed before the statute of limitations ran.

(D) No, because the attorney returned the $1,000 retainer to the passenger.

Question 30.

An attorney filed a personal injury suit on behalf of a plaintiff. The defendant was personally served with process. The attorney knows that the defendant is insured by an insurance company and that another attorney has been retained by the insurance company to represent the defendant. No responsive pleading has been filed on behalf of the defendant, and the time for filing expired over 10 days ago.

Is the attorney subject to discipline if the attorney proceeds to have a default judgment entered?

(A) Yes, because the attorney knows that another attorney had been retained by the insurance company to represent the defendant.

(B) Yes, because the attorney failed to extend professional courtesy to another lawyer.

(C) No, because the attorney is properly representing her client's interests.

(D) No, because any judgment will be satisfied by the insurance company.

Question 31.

An attorney is a candidate in a contested election for judicial office. Her opponent is the incumbent judge and has occupied the bench for many years. The director of the state commission on judicial conduct, upon inquiry by the attorney, erroneously told the attorney that the judge had been reprimanded by the commission for misconduct in office. The attorney, who had confidence in the director, believed him. In fact, the judge had not been reprimanded by the commission; the commission had conducted hearings on the judge's alleged misconduct in office and, by a three-to-two vote, declined to reprimand the judge.

Decisions of the commission, including reprimands, are not confidential. Is the attorney subject to discipline for publicly stating that the judge had been reprimanded for misconduct?

(A) Yes, because the official records of the commission would have disclosed the truth.

(B) Yes, because the judge had not been reprimanded.

(C) No, because the attorney reasonably relied on the director's information.

(D) No, because the judge was a candidate in a contested election.

Question 32.

An attorney is a well-known, highly skilled litigator. The attorney's practice is in an area of law in which the trial proceedings are heard by the court without a jury.

In an interview with a prospective client, the attorney said, "I make certain that I give the campaign committee of every candidate for elective judicial office more money than any other lawyer gives, whether it's $500 or $5,000. Judges know who helps them get elected." The prospective client did not retain the attorney.

Is the attorney subject to discipline?

(A) Yes, if the attorney's contributions are made without consideration of candidates' merits.

(B) Yes, because the attorney implied that the attorney receives favored treatment by judges.

(C) No, if the attorney's statements were true.

(D) No, because the prospective client did not retain the attorney.

Question 33.

A judge is presiding in a case that has, as its main issue, a complicated point of commercial law. The lawyers have not presented the case to the judge's satisfaction, and the judge believes she needs additional legal advice.
The judge's former partner in law practice is an attorney and an expert in the field of law that is at issue. The attorney has no interest in the case.

Is it proper for the judge to consult the attorney?

(A) Yes, because the attorney has no interest in the case.

(B) Yes, if the judge believes that the attorney's advice is needed to serve the interests of justice.

(C) No, unless all parties in the case first give their written consent to the judge's consultation with the attorney.

(D) No, unless the judge informs the parties of the attorney's identity and the substance of the attorney's advice, and asks for their responses.

Question 34.

Under a state law, the court's appointment of lawyers as special masters in certain proceedings is discretionary with the court. A judge decided to appoint special masters in all such proceedings, regardless of their nature and complexity, and decided that compensation for such appointees would be at a reasonable hourly rate. The judge believed that this practice would ensure competent and impartial handling of every proceeding. The judge further decided to use published law directories to compile a list of qualified prospective appointees.

Is the judge's proposed practice proper?

(A) Yes, because it results in competent and impartial handling of the proceedings.

(B) Yes, because the appointees will be compensated at a reasonable hourly rate.

(C) No, because the practice may result in unnecessary appointments.

(D) No, because the judge cannot use law directories to compile a list of qualified prospective appointees.

Question 35.

A trust company entered into the following arrangement with an attorney who was newly admitted to the bar:

The trust company would provide the attorney with free office space in the building in which the trust company had its offices. If a customer of the trust company contacted the trust company about a trust or will, an officer of the trust company, who would not be a lawyer, would advise the customer and help the customer work out the details of the trust or will. The customer would be informed that the necessary documents would be prepared by the trust company's staff. The completed documents would be submitted by an officer of the trust company to the customer for execution.

The attorney, in accordance with a memorandum from the trust company's trust officer detailing the plan, would prepare the necessary documents. The attorney would never meet with the customer and would not charge the customer for these services. The attorney would be free to engage in private practice, subject only to the limitation that the attorney could not accept employment adverse to the trust company.

Is the attorney subject to discipline for entering into the arrangement with the trust company?

(A) Yes, because the attorney is restricting his right to practice.

(B) Yes, because the attorney is aiding the trust company in the practice of law.

(C) No, because the attorney is not charging the customer for his services.

(D) No, because the attorney is not giving advice to the trust company's customers.

Question 36.

An attorney represented a husband and wife in the purchase of a business financed by contributions from their respective separate funds. The business was jointly operated by the husband and wife after acquisition. After several years, a dispute arose over the management of the business. The husband and wife sought the attorney's advice, and the matter was settled on the basis of an agreement drawn by the attorney and signed by the husband and wife. Later, the wife asked the attorney to represent her in litigation against her husband based on the claim that her husband was guilty of fraud and misrepresentation in the negotiations for the prior settlement agreement.

Is it proper for the attorney to represent the wife in this matter?

(A) Yes, if all information relevant to the litigation was received by the attorney in the presence of both the husband and wife.

(B) Yes, if there is reason to believe the husband misled both the wife and the attorney at the time of the prior agreement.

(C) No, because the attorney had previously acted for both parties in reaching the agreement now in dispute.

(D) No, unless the husband is now represented by independent counsel.

Question 37.

A client retained an attorney to recover for a personal injury. In the retainer agreement signed by the client and the attorney, the client agreed to cooperate fully and pay the attorney a contingent fee computed as a percentage of the amount of recovery after expenses: 25 percent if settled before trial, 30 percent if settled before verdict, 35 percent after verdict, and 40 percent after appeal.

The attorney's representation of the client in the matter extended over a three-year period, during which the attorney advanced a large amount for litigation expenses. After trial, the client obtained a jury verdict for an amount larger than either the attorney or the client had anticipated. However, the defendant filed an appeal based on questions of evidence and the measure of damages. Meanwhile, the defendant made an offer of settlement for approximately the amount the attorney had originally projected as reasonable to expect. The client, who was hard-pressed financially, directed the attorney to accept the offer and settle. The attorney refused, because she was confident that there was no reversible error in the trial and that the appeal was without merit. The attorney reasonably believed that the appeal was filed solely to gain negotiating advantage in settlement negotiations.

Is the attorney subject to discipline?

(A) Yes, because the attorney's percentage under the fee contract increased after appeal.

(B) Yes, because the client directed the attorney to accept the settlement offer.

(C) No, because the decision whether to settle or defend an appeal is a tactical matter for the attorney to determine.

(D) No, because evaluation of the merits of an appeal requires the exercise of independent professional judgment.

Question 38.

An attorney advertises on the local television station. In the advertisements, a professional actor says:

"Do you need a lawyer? Call 555-555-5555. Her fees might be lower than you think."

The attorney approved the prerecorded advertisement and is keeping in her office files a copy of the recording of the actual transmission and a record of when each transmission was made.

Is the advertisement proper?

(A) Yes.

(B) No, unless the attorney's fees are lower than those generally charged in the area where she practices.

(C) No, because she used a professional actor for the television advertisement.

(D) No, if she makes a charge for the initial consultation.

Question 39.

An attorney represented both the owner of an art gallery and a publisher. The gallery owner and the publisher each made a practice of paying the attorney's fees in cash. The attorney received separate cash payments from the gallery owner and the publisher on the same day. Each payment consisted of 10 $100 bills, which the attorney immediately deposited in her bank account. One week later, the attorney was contacted by United States Treasury agents, who informed her that four of the bills had been identified as counterfeit. The agents did not accuse the attorney of knowingly passing the counterfeit money, but asked her who had given her the bills. The attorney was subpoenaed to testify before a grand jury and was asked who could have given her the counterfeit money.

Is it proper for the attorney to provide the grand jury with the names of the gallery owner and the publisher?

(A) Yes, because negotiation of a counterfeit bill is a criminal act.

(B) Yes, because under the circumstances neither client's identity is privileged.

(C) No, because counterfeiting is not a crime that involves an imminent threat of death or serious bodily harm.

(D) No, because the attorney has no way of knowing which of the two clients gave her the counterfeit bills.

Question 40.

A corporation has applied to a bank for a $900,000 loan to be secured by a lien on the corporation's inventory. The inventory, consisting of small items, constantly turns over. The security documents are complex and if improperly drawn they could result in an invalid lien. The bank has approved the loan on the condition that the corporation and the bank jointly retain an attorney to prepare the necessary security instruments and that the corporation pay the attorney's fees. Both the corporation and the bank gave informed consent in writing to the attorney's representation of both parties. This arrangement is customary in the city in which the attorney's law office and the bank are located. It is obvious to the attorney that he can adequately represent the interests of both the corporation and the bank.

Is it proper for the attorney to prepare the security documents under these circumstances?

(A) Yes, because both the bank and the corporation have given their informed consent to the arrangement.

(B) Yes, because the arrangement is customary in the community.

(C) No, because the attorney's fees are being paid by the corporation, not the bank.

(D) No, because the corporation and the bank have differing interests.

Question 41.

An attorney agreed to represent a client who was being prosecuted for driving while intoxicated in a jurisdiction in which there is an increased penalty for a second offense. The client told the attorney that his driver's license had been obtained under an assumed name because his prior license had been suspended for driving while under the influence of alcohol. The client asked the attorney not to disclose his true name during the course of the representation and told the attorney that, if called as a witness, he would give his assumed name. The attorney informed the client that, in order to properly defend the case, the attorney must call the client as a witness.

The attorney called the client as a witness and, in response to the attorney's question "What is your name?", the client gave his assumed name.

Is the attorney subject to discipline?

(A) Yes, because the attorney knowingly used false testimony.

(B) Yes, if the client committed a felony when he obtained the driver's license under an assumed name.

(C) No, because the attorney's knowledge of the client's true name was obtained during the course of representation.

(D) No, unless the client's true name is an issue in the proceeding.

Question 42.

A judge is one of three trustees of a trust for the educational benefit of her grandchildren. The trust owns 5,000 shares of stock in a large oil company. The stock has been selling for the past year at $10,000 a share. The oil company is suing a refining company for breach of an oil refining agreement, and the case is assigned to the judge for trial. The judge believes that she can be fair and impartial.

Must the judge disqualify herself from the case?

(A) Yes, because the trust has more than a de minimis financial interest in the oil company.

(B) Yes, unless the outcome of the lawsuit is unlikely to affect the value of the stock.

(C) No, unless the judge personally owns stock in either party to the litigation.

(D) No, because the judge believes she can remain impartial.

Question 43.

A judge has served for many years as a director of a charitable organization that maintains a camp for disadvantaged children, although she has not received any compensation for her services. The organization has never been involved in litigation. The charity has decided to sponsor a public testimonial dinner in the judge's honor. As part of the occasion, the local bar association intends to commission and present to the judge her portrait at a cost of $4,000.

The money to pay for the portrait will come from a "public testimonial fund" that will be raised by the city's bar association from contributions of lawyers who are members of the association and who practice in the city's courts.

Is it proper for the judge to accept the gift of the portrait?

(A) Yes, because the gift is incident to a public testimonial for the judge.

(B) Yes, because the judge did not receive compensation for her services to the charitable organization.

(C) No, because the cost of the gift exceeds $1,000.

(D) No, because the funds for the gift are contributed by lawyers who practice in the city's courts.

Question 44.

An attorney, who had represented a client for many years, prepared the client's will and acted as one of the two subscribing witnesses to its execution. The will gave 10 percent of the client's estate to the client's housekeeper, 10 percent to the client's son and sole heir, and the residue to charity. Upon the client's death one year later, the executor of the will asked the attorney to represent him in probating the will and administering the estate. At that time, the executor informed the attorney that the client's son had notified him that he would contest the probate of the will on the grounds that the client lacked the required mental capacity at the time the will was executed. The attorney believes that the client was fully competent at all times and will so testify, if called as a witness. The other subscribing witness to the client's will predeceased the client.

Is it proper for the attorney to represent the executor in the probate of the will?

(A) Yes, because the attorney is the sole surviving witness to the execution of the will.

(B) Yes, because the attorney's testimony will support the validity of the will.

(C) No, because the attorney will be called to testify on a contested issue of fact.

(D) No, because the attorney will be representing an interest adverse to the client's heir at law.

Question 45.

An attorney represented a buyer in a real estate transaction. Due to the attorney's negligence in drafting the purchase agreement, the buyer was required to pay for a survey that should have been paid by the seller. The attorney fully disclosed this negligence to the buyer, and the buyer suggested that he would be satisfied if the attorney simply reimbursed the buyer for the entire cost of the survey.

Although the buyer might have recovered additional damages if a malpractice action were filed, the attorney reasonably believed that the proposed settlement was fair to the buyer. Accordingly, in order to forestall a malpractice action, the attorney readily agreed to make the reimbursement. The attorney drafted a settlement agreement, and it was executed by both the attorney and the buyer.

Was the attorney's conduct proper?

(A) Yes, if the attorney advised the buyer in writing that the buyer should seek independent representation before deciding to enter into the settlement agreement.

(B) Yes, because the attorney reasonably believed that the proposed settlement was fair to the buyer.

(C) No, because the attorney settled a case involving liability for malpractice while the matter was still ongoing.

(D) No, unless the buyer was separately represented in negotiating and finalizing the settlement agreement.

Question 46.

An attorney represented a plaintiff in a civil suit against a defendant who was represented by other counsel. In the course of developing the plaintiff's case, the attorney discovered evidence that she reasonably believed showed that the defendant had committed a crime. The attorney felt that the defendant's crime should be reported to local prosecutorial authorities. After full disclosure, the plaintiff consented to the attorney's doing so. Without advising the defendant's counsel, the attorney informed the local prosecutor of her findings, but she sought no advantage in the civil suit from her actions. The defendant was subsequently indicted, tried, and acquitted of the offense.

Was the attorney's disclosure to prosecutorial authorities proper?

(A) Yes, because the attorney reasonably believed the defendant was guilty of a crime.

(B) Yes, because the attorney was required to report knowledge of criminal conduct when that knowledge was obtained through unprivileged sources.

(C) No, because the attorney did not advise the other counsel of her disclosure before making it.

(D) No, because the plaintiff's civil suit against the defendant was still pending.

Question 47.

A witness was subpoenaed to appear and testify at a state legislative committee hearing. The witness retained an attorney to represent her at the hearing. During the hearing, the attorney, reasonably believing that it was in the witness's best interest not to answer, advised the witness not to answer certain questions on the grounds that she had a constitutional right not to answer. The committee chairperson directed the witness to answer and cautioned her that refusal to answer was a misdemeanor and that criminal prosecution would be instituted if she did not answer.

Upon the attorney's advice, the witness persisted in her refusal to answer. The witness was subsequently convicted for her refusal to answer.

Is the attorney subject to discipline?

(A) Yes, because his advice to the witness was not legally sound.

(B) Yes, because the witness, in acting on the attorney's advice, committed a crime.

(C) No, if the offense the witness committed did not involve moral turpitude.

(D) No, if the attorney reasonably believed the witness had a legal right to refuse to answer the questions.

Question 48.

An attorney hired a recent law school graduate as an associate. For the first six months, the associate was assigned to draft legal documents that the attorney carefully reviewed and revised before filing. However, shortly after the associate was admitted to the bar, the attorney told the associate that he would be going on vacation the following week and was assigning her the representation of the landlord in a housing case that was going to trial while he was away. The associate had never conducted or observed a trial before and, because she had not previously worked on any housing cases, she was unfamiliar with the relevant law and procedure. She did not believe that she would have enough time to learn everything that she needed to know, but she was reluctant to decline the assignment. Before the trial began, she met with the landlord and disclosed that this would be her first trial, but the landlord did not object. Although the associate prepared diligently, the landlord lost the trial.

Is the attorney subject to discipline?

(A) Yes, because the attorney did not ensure that the associate was competent to conduct the trial on her own.

(B) Yes, because the landlord lost at trial.

(C) No, because the attorney could reasonably assume that, having been admitted to the bar, the associate was capable of conducting the trial.

(D) No, because the landlord did not object to the associate's representation.

Question 49.

An attorney currently represents a builder who is the plaintiff in a suit to recover for breach of a contract to build a house. The builder also has pending before the zoning commission a petition to rezone property the builder owns. However, the builder is represented by another attorney in the zoning matter.

A neighbor who owns property adjoining that of the builder has asked the attorney to represent him in opposing the builder's petition for rezoning. The neighbor knows that the attorney represents the builder in the contract action.

Is it proper for the attorney to represent the neighbor in the zoning matter?

(A) Yes, if there is no common issue of law or fact between the two matters.

(B) Yes, because one matter is a judicial proceeding and the other is an administrative proceeding.

(C) No, because the attorney is currently representing the builder in the contract action.

(D) No, if there is a possibility that both matters will be appealed to the same court.

Question 50.

An elected prosecutor plans to run for reelection in six months. Last year, two teenage girls were kidnapped from a shopping center and sexually assaulted. The community was in an uproar about the crime and put pressure on the prosecutor to indict and convict the assailant. Four months ago, a suspect was arrested and charged with the crimes. The trial is scheduled to begin next week.

The prosecutor met with the police chief last week to review the evidence in the case. At that time, the prosecutor first learned that, before they were interviewed by the detective in charge of sexual assault crimes, the two victims had been tape-recorded discussing the case between themselves in an interview room. Reviewing the tape, the prosecutor realized that the girls' descriptions of the assailant differed significantly in terms of height, weight, and hair color. When officially interviewed, however, their descriptions matched almost perfectly.

The suspect's appointed counsel was busy handling a large caseload of indigent defendants and neglected to seek access to the prosecution's investigative file. The prosecutor was virtually certain that suspect's counsel was unaware of the tape recording. Given the other evidence in the case, the prosecutor reasonably believed that the girls accurately identified the suspect as their assailant. The prosecutor did not reveal the existence of the tape to defense counsel.

Is the prosecutor subject to discipline?

(A) Yes, because the tape raises a legitimate question about the victims' eyewitness identification of the suspect as the assailant.

(B) Yes, unless the prosecutor reasonably believed that the girls accurately identified the suspect as their assailant.

(C) No, because under the adversary system of criminal justice, it is expected that each party will marshal the evidence best supporting its own position.

(D) No, unless the suspect's counsel submitted a request for all mitigating or exculpatory evidence before the start of trial.

Question 51.

An attorney represented the plaintiff in an automobile accident case. Two weeks before the date set for trial, the attorney discovered that there was an eyewitness to the accident. The attorney interviewed the witness. Her version of the accident was contrary to that of the plaintiff and, if believed by the trier of fact, would establish that the plaintiff was at fault. The witness told the attorney that she had not been interviewed by defense counsel.

The witness also told the attorney that she was uncomfortable with testifying and that she had been thinking about taking a vacation to Europe the following week. The attorney told the witness that, since no one had subpoenaed her yet, she had no obligation to appear. He told her that trials were very difficult for witnesses and suggested that she take the vacation so that she would be unavailable to testify.

Is the attorney subject to discipline?

(A) Yes, because the attorney asked the witness to leave the jurisdiction.

(B) Yes, because the attorney did not subpoena the witness knowing she was an eyewitness.

(C) No, because the witness had not been subpoenaed by the defense.

(D) No, because the attorney did not offer the witness any inducement not to appear at the trial.

Question 52.

An attorney represented the plaintiff in a personal injury matter. The attorney had heard that the defendant in the matter was anxious to settle the case and reasonably believed that the defendant's lawyer had not informed the defendant about the attorney's recent offer of settlement. The attorney instructed her non-lawyer investigator to tell the defendant about the settlement offer so that the attorney could be sure that the defendant's lawyer did not force the case to trial merely to increase the defendant's lawyer's fee.

Is the attorney subject to discipline?

(A) Yes, because the defendant was represented by counsel.

(B) Yes, because the attorney was assisting the investigator in the unauthorized practice of law.

(C) No, because the investigator is not a lawyer.

(D) No, because the attorney reasonably believed that the defendant's lawyer was not keeping the defendant informed.

Question 53.

An attorney was approached by a husband and a wife who had decided to dissolve their marriage. They had no children and had worked out a tentative mutual property settlement. They did not want to retain separate lawyers because they hoped to save money and believed that working with one attorney was more likely to result in a reasonably amicable dissolution. Before coming to the attorney, they had drafted and each had signed a written agreement not to run up the costs and increase the adversarial nature of the dissolution by retaining separate lawyers.

The attorney believed that he was able to provide competent and diligent representation to both the husband and the wife. The attorney consulted with both independently concerning the implications of the common representation, including the advantages and risks involved and the effect on their respective attorney-client privileges. The attorney reduced the disclosures to writing in the form of a written retainer agreement and gave them each several days to consult independent legal counsel if they so desired. The husband and the wife each chose not to consult independent counsel.

After six months of reasonably amicable negotiations, the wife announced that she had changed her mind about the representation and had decided to retain her own lawyer. However, after the husband and the attorney insisted that she was obligated to adhere to her prior written agreement, she reluctantly agreed to abide by it. The attorney was then able to draft a property settlement agreement satisfactory to both parties.

Is the attorney subject to discipline for his conduct in the representation?

(A) Yes, because the attorney should not have undertaken to represent both the husband and the wife in the first place.

(B) Yes, because the attorney insisted that the wife not hire another lawyer.

(C) No, because both the husband and the wife initially consented to all aspects of the representation.

(D) No, because the husband and the wife independently made the agreement that neither would retain separate counsel.

Question 54.

An attorney is a well-known tax lawyer and author. During congressional hearings on tax reform, the attorney testified to her personal belief and expert opinion on the pending reform package. She failed to disclose in her testimony that she was being compensated by a private client for her appearance. In her testimony, the attorney took the position favored by her client, but the position was also one that the attorney believed was in the public interest.

Was it proper for the attorney to present this testimony without identifying her private client?

(A) Yes, because the attorney believed that the position she advocated was in the public interest.

(B) Yes, because Congress is interested in the content of the testimony and not who is paying the witness.

(C) No, because a lawyer may not accept a fee for trying to influence legislative action.

(D) No, because a lawyer who appears in a legislative hearing should identify the capacity in which the lawyer appeals.

Question 55.

An attorney closed her law practice when she became a state senator. A bank, one of the senator's former private clients, asked her as its senator to try to persuade a state agency to grant the bank a license to open a new branch bank. While the bank's request was pending before the agency, the senator wrote a letter on her legislative letterhead to the agency's chair, asserting that the branch would satisfy a local business need and urging that the bank's application be granted. The senator neither sought nor received any compensation from the bank for her efforts. Eventually the agency granted the bank's application, in part because of the senator's efforts.

Is the senator subject to discipline?

(A) Yes, because the senator used her public position to influence the agency on behalf of the bank.

(B) Yes, because the agency granted the bank's application in part due to the senator's efforts.

(C) No, because the senator's letter to the agency's chair did not express an opinion about the law.

(D) No, because the senator acted on behalf of the bank as a constituent and not as a client.

Question 56.

A county law prohibits stores from selling alcoholic beverages before noon on Sundays. Failure to comply is a misdemeanor punishable by a fine of $150.

An attorney was hired by a client who owns several liquor stores. The client asked the attorney whether any store owners had been prosecuted for violating the law and whether the fine could be imposed for every sale on a Sunday before noon or only for every Sunday on which alcohol was sold before noon. The client also asked what he could do to minimize the risk that he would be detected.

The attorney accurately told the client that the fine could only be imposed for each Sunday on which he sold alcoholic beverages before noon, not for each transaction, and that no one had been prosecuted under the law as yet. She also told him that she thought it would be improper to advise him about how to avoid detection. The client thanked the attorney for the information and hung up. Several weeks later, the attorney learned that the client had begun to open his store for business on Sundays at 9 a.m.

Is the attorney subject to discipline?

(A) Yes, because the attorney reasonably should have known that the information she gave the client would encourage him to violate the law.

(B) Yes, because the attorney did not discourage her client from breaking the law.

(C) No, because the attorney merely gave the client her honest opinion about the consequences that were likely to result if he violated the law.

(D) No, because the lawyer and the client could have discussed the best way to avoid detection under the criminal law.

Question 57.

A judge has served on a trial court of general jurisdiction for almost three years. During that time, he was assigned criminal cases almost exclusively. Several months ago, however, the judge was assigned an interesting case involving a constitutional challenge to a statute recently passed by the state legislature. The statute permitted any local public school district with an overcrowding problem to purchase educational services for its students in any other public or private school within 15 miles.

Although the briefs submitted by the parties were excellent, the judge was not confident that he had a good grasp of the issues in the case. Accordingly, he took one of his more experienced colleagues on the trial court out to lunch and discussed the case with her in great detail. The colleague was far more conservative than the judge, but he agreed with her and eventually ruled in accord with her views. The case is now on appeal.

Is the judge subject to discipline?

(A) Yes, because the judge sought an ex parte communication on the merits of a case pending before him.

(B) Yes, because the judge initiated a discussion with a colleague that may have influenced his judgment in the case.

(C) No, because the judge is permitted to obtain the advice of a disinterested expert on the law.

(D) No, because the judge was permitted to consult about a pending case with another judge.

Question 58.

An attorney is a senior partner at a law firm in which there are 50 lawyers. The firm pays each of its lawyers a fixed annual salary. In addition, at year's end, each lawyer receives a bonus from the profits of the firm in proportion to the annual salary of each and its relation to the total of the fixed annual salaries of all lawyers.

The attorney plans to introduce a new management plan under which the firm's non-lawyer office administrator would have general charge of all business matters but would not participate in any decisions involving legal judgment. The administrator would be paid a fixed annual salary and would be included as a participant in the firm's bonus plan on the same basis as the lawyers in the firm. This would usually yield a bonus of approximately one-fourth to one-third of the administrator's total annual compensation. The amount paid to the administrator will not exceed the compensation commonly paid to law office administrators within the local legal community.

Is it proper for the attorney to institute such a plan?

(A) Yes, because the amount paid to the administrator does not exceed the compensation commonly paid to law office administrators within the local legal community.

(B) Yes, because an employee of the firm may be compensated based on the profits of the firm.

(C) No, because the administrator's bonus is computed on the same basis as those of the lawyers in the firm.

(D) No, because the administrator's compensation is derived from the legal fees of the firm's lawyers.

Question 59.

An attorney represented a client in an action against the client's former partner to recover damages for breach of contract. During the representation, the client presented the attorney with incontrovertible proof that the former partner had committed perjury in a prior action that was resolved in the partner's favor. Neither the attorney nor the client was involved in any way in the prior action. The attorney believes that it would be detrimental to the client's best interests to reveal the perjury because of the implication that might be drawn from the former close personal and business relationship between the client and the former partner.

Would it be proper for the attorney to fail to disclose the perjury to the tribunal?

(A) No, because the information is unprivileged.

(B) No, because the attorney has knowledge that the former partner perpetrated a fraud on the tribunal.

(C) Yes, because neither the client nor the attorney was involved in the prior action.

(D) Yes, because the attorney believes that the disclosure would be detrimental to the client's best interests.

Question 60.

An attorney represented 10 plaintiffs in a case against a railroad in which the plaintiffs were injured when a train derailed. The railroad offered the attorney a $500,000 lump sum settlement for the 10 plaintiffs. The attorney allocated the $500,000 among the 10 plaintiffs with the amount paid each plaintiff dependent on the nature and extent of that plaintiff's injuries. The attorney reasonably believed the division was fair to each plaintiff.

The railroad would not settle any of the claims unless all were settled. The attorney told each plaintiff the total amount the railroad was prepared to pay, the amount that the individual would receive, and the basis on which that amount was calculated. The attorney did not tell any plaintiff the amount to be received by any other plaintiff. The attorney believed that if she revealed to each plaintiff the amount of each individual settlement, it might jeopardize the settlement.

Each of the plaintiffs agreed to his or her settlement amount and was satisfied with that amount.

Is the attorney subject to discipline for entering into this settlement?

(A) Yes, because the attorney was aiding the lawyer for the railroad in making a lump sum settlement.

(B) Yes, because no individual plaintiff knew the amount to be received by any other plaintiff.

(C) No, because disclosing all settlements to each plaintiff might have jeopardized the entire settlement.

(D) No, because the attorney reasonably believed that the division was fair and each plaintiff agreed to his or her settlement and was satisfied with the amount.

B. Answers to Model Questions

Question 1.

B is the correct answer. A lawyer must provide competent representation to clients. Model Rule 1.1. Competent representation requires having the legal knowledge and skill necessary for the representation. To maintain the required level of knowledge and skill, a lawyer should keep abreast of changes in the law through continuing study and education, as well as comply with any continuing education requirements to which the lawyer is subject. Model Rule 1.1, Comment [6]. Independent study is just as valid as continuing legal education courses in maintaining the attorney's competence, although failure to attend continuing legal education courses would be improper if the state required him to do so.

A is incorrect. The attorney must maintain competence without regard to the cost of doing so. Additionally, the word "unless" implies that continuing legal education courses are the only way for the attorney to maintain his competence.

C is incorrect. As stated above, continuing legal education courses are not the only way the attorney can maintain his competence.

D is incorrect. Being insured against malpractice has nothing to do with a lawyer's duty to maintain the legal knowledge and skills needed to provide competent representation.

Question 2.

C is the correct answer. Under Model Rule 1.1, an attorney must have the legal knowledge and skill necessary for the representation. In determining whether an attorney has the requisite knowledge and skill in a particular matter, relevant factors include the relative complexity and specialized nature of the matter, the attorney's general experience, the attorney's training and experience in the field in question, the preparation and study the attorney is able to give the matter, and whether it is feasible to refer the matter to, or associate or consult with, an attorney of established competence in the field in question. The standard of competence is usually that of a general practitioner, unless the attorney claims to be an expert in a particular area of law. Here, it appears that the corporation retained the firm because the partner held himself out as an expert in securities regulation law, a complex and specialized area of the law, and the attorney, a newly minted attorney, specifically stated he did not have the time to prepare himself to handle the matter competently. Consequently, the attorney would be in violation of the rule if he continues to represent the corporation without the required level of competence, and the partner would be in violation of the rule for directing him to do so and failing to give the attorney proper supervision.

A is incorrect. Although the attorney is a member of the bar and therefore licensed to practice law, he is admittedly incompetent to handle this particular representation without assistance from an attorney who is competent in this area. Consequently, the partner is in violation for directing the attorney to represent the corporation without any assistance.

B is incorrect. Under Model Rule 1.16(b)(6), an attorney may withdraw from a case if working on it would cause unreasonable financial hardship on the attorney. However, the partner willingly accepted the corporation as a client, and the mere fact the partner "prefers" to work on cases with larger fee potential would not meet the standard for withdrawal.

D is incorrect. If the assignment is appropriate, a client generally does not need to give permission for an attorney to assign that representation to an associate. However, because a client's consent does not excuse incompetent representation, the representation would be improper even if the corporation had given permission to assign the matter to the attorney.

Question 3.

A is the correct answer. Model Rule 8.4 defines the acts that constitute misconduct by a lawyer. Model Rule 8.4(c) describes as professional misconduct any conduct "involving dishonesty, fraud, deceit or misrepresentation." The definition is not limited to misconduct in connection with the practice of law but, under Comment [2], extends to all offenses that "indicate lack of those characteristics relevant to law practice," including violence, dishonesty, and breach of trust. Also, misconduct is misconduct wherever it occurs — whether in the state in which the attorney is licensed to practice or elsewhere. Here, the attorney has knowingly filed a false financial statement in connection with a professional license application, a clear violation of the Rule.

B is incorrect. The definition of misconduct extends far beyond conviction for a criminal offense. Comment [2] to Model Rule 8.4 states, "Many kinds of illegal conduct reflect adversely on fitness to practice law, such as offenses involving fraud and the offense of willful failure to file an income tax return."

C is incorrect. A lawyer is judged not only by his or her conduct in his or her capacity as lawyer, but by all conduct that measures his or her honesty, trustworthiness, and general fitness as a lawyer. See Model Rule 8.4(b).

D is incorrect. Geography has nothing to do with the concept of misconduct. Misconduct is misconduct wherever it occurs.

Question 4.

D is the correct answer. Lawyers are prohibited from soliciting business from prospective clients by in-person contact or live telephone contact. Model Rule 7.3. The key word is "prospective" — that is, "future" clients. The prohibition against solicitation does not extend to persons with whom the lawyer has had a prior personal or professional relationship, "or in situations in which the lawyer is motivated by considerations other than the lawyer's pecuniary gain." Model Rule 7.3, Comment [4]. Consequently, the prohibition does not extend to contacts with former clients, personal friends, or family members. Here, the attorney is dealing with a former client whose interests may be adversely affected if the attorney does not advise her of the new IRS regulation. Under the facts, you can assume that the attorney was motivated not by a desire for pecuniary gain but by a good-faith instinct to help a former client, but in any event, it's enough that the woman is a former client.

A is incorrect. The attorney is permitted to contact the woman as a former client whether or not she has reason to believe her former client has another attorney. The attorney has no way of knowing whether her former client has another attorney or if the other attorney is a specialist in tax law or is even aware of the new regulation. The Rule does not require the attorney to inquire into these facts.

B is incorrect. The test is not whether the person is a current client but whether the person is a former client. For purposes of Model Rule 7.3, once a client always a client.

C is incorrect. The attorney is free to offer and supply her services to her client in any way her former client may be willing to utilize them. The issue here is solicitation, not limits on the scope of representation.

Question 5.

D is the correct answer. The answer recognizes the three basic principles a lawyer must observe when dealing with client funds: (1) client funds must always be kept separate from the lawyer's funds in a designated clients' escrow account; (2) as soon as the client's interest in the funds is fixed, the client's money must be delivered to the client; and (3) if both the client and the attorney claim any interest in any part of the funds — for example, if a dispute arises as to the lawyer's fees — the funds must remain in the separate client account until there is an accounting and their respective interests can be severed. Model Rule 1.15. Here, the attorney's maximum claim was for fees totaling 6 hours × $50 = $300. When the bail hearing was completed, the client's interest in the advance was $500. The attorney had a duty to return this promptly. Because the client had demanded $800, the lawyer's fee of $300 was in dispute. Consequently, the money representing the fee had to be retained in the Clients' Fund Account until the dispute was resolved.

A is incorrect. The funds in dispute totaled only $300. The balance of $500 was not in dispute and belonged to the client when it was not applied to the bail costs. The attorney was under a duty to return $500 to the client because the money was not used for the purpose intended.

B is incorrect. Because the fee of $300 was in dispute, the attorney had no right to transfer that sum to his fee account. He was required to retain the funds in his Clients' Fund Account until the dispute was resolved. Further, the attorney had no right to retain the balance of $500 in either account pending the appeal. The money was deposited with the attorney only in connection with the bail application, not the appeal itself.

C is incorrect. The attorney was right to send the $500 to the client, but wrong in transferring $300 to his fee account. So long as his fee was in dispute, the $300 had to be retained in the Clients' Fund Account. Model Rule 1.15(e).

Question 6.

B is the correct answer. A judge is expected to perform his or her duties fairly, impartially, and without prejudice against any litigant. Model Code of Judicial Conduct, Rule 2.2. The test is the judge's mindset as perceived by a reasonable observer. If the judge has a personal bias toward a party or his or her lawyer, or personal knowledge of disputed evidentiary facts concerning the proceeding, he or she must disqualify himself or herself. Also, if he or she or a former law partner has served either side as a lawyer concerning the matter, or if he or she has served as a material witness in the matter, he or she must disqualify himself or herself. B correctly states the issue facing the judge. If there is any chance that his prior investigation of the defendant will prejudice his judgment, he must disqualify himself.

A is incorrect because it misstates the test for disqualification. It doesn't matter that the prior investigation is unrelated to the present case. The relevant question is whether the judge is adversely influenced by his participation in the investigation.

C is incorrect. Although it states a basis for suspecting prejudice by the judge against the defendant, it is not as good an answer as B, which correctly frames the issue as one of potential prejudice.

D is incorrect. This option does not revolve around the judge's state of mind. It is just as reasonable to conclude that the judge was not prejudiced by the prior investigation as that he was prejudiced. The issue is whether he was and is actually prejudiced against the defendant. B is the best formula for deciding that issue.

Question 7.

B is the correct answer. When a lawyer gives a client advice, he or she may rely on considerations other than those involved in giving purely technical legal advice. Model Rule 2.1. Consequently, it is proper for a lawyer to rely on moral, economic, and social factors in doing so, which is what the attorney did here.

A is incorrect because the issue isn't whether the landlord accepted the attorney's advice — and, in fact, a lawyer should not be deterred from giving candid advice simply because the client might not be happy about it — but whether the attorney acted properly in going beyond the technical legal aspect of the case in advising the landlord.

C is incorrect. An initial, or engagement, letter to the client is concerned with fees. Its purpose is to make clear what services the lawyer will provide and what he or she will charge for them, not in what form he or she will render advice. Model Rule 1.5.

D is incorrect. It raises the issue of a lawyer's responsibility to "act with . . . zeal in advocacy." Model Rule 1.3, Comment [1]. But that isn't really the issue here. The issue is what is the proper scope for the advice a lawyer gives a client. Not only is it proper for a lawyer to refer to considerations other than the law in advising a client, he or she also has a responsibility to exercise independent professional judgment in advising a client and to advise the client in a straightforward, honest manner, in the best interests of the client. Here, the attorney has done exactly that.

Question 8.

B is the correct answer. Basic to the integrity of the legal profession is the principle that only persons admitted to the practice of law may provide legal services to others. Consequently, any person who is not a lawyer but who gives legal advice is said to engage in the unauthorized practice of law, and any lawyer who helps a non-lawyer to engage in the unauthorized practice of law violates Model Rule 5.5(a). Here, the bank is not authorized to practice law, but it is providing legal services through its salaried employee, the attorney. Thus, the attorney is assisting the bank in the unauthorized practice of law.

A is incorrect. A newsletter does not provide legal "advice" to any particular person, but only supplies generalized legal information to the general public. Even so, a lawyer is not prevented from giving advice to a non-client. However, if the lawyer is representing a client whose interests may be affected by the non-client's actions, the lawyer is required to avoid stating or implying to the non-client that the lawyer is disinterested. In that case, if the lawyer knows or reasonably should know that the unrepresented person misunderstands the lawyer's role in the matter, he or she must make reasonable efforts to correct the misunderstanding. Model Rule 4.3.

C is incorrect. Whether the attorney charges a fee or not, he's still assisting the bank in the unauthorized practice of law.

D is incorrect. Only a lawyer is subject to discipline under the Model Rules. Consequently, the attorney is subject to discipline *because* he is a member of the bar.

Question 9.

A is the correct answer. Although the attorney does not have the "requisite knowledge and skill" to competently represent his cousin and knows he doesn't, this scenario would fall under the "emergency" situation discussed in Model Rule 1.1, Comment [3]. When his cousin called, it would have been impractical for the attorney to refer his cousin to another lawyer or to consult with another lawyer, so he gave reasonably necessary assistance to get his cousin out on bail. However, for any additional work, the attorney would have to become competent or find another lawyer to take on the matter, which the attorney did in this case.

B is incorrect. The fact that the attorney and his cousin are related has nothing to do with whether the attorney can represent his cousin competently. The attorney must decide whether he has the requisite knowledge and skill to provide his cousin with competent representation regardless of their relationship.

C is incorrect. It is precisely because of the attorney's inexperience that he made the decision that he did. He acted appropriately in giving assistance in an "emergency" situation, which included finding an experienced criminal lawyer for his cousin.

D is incorrect. The attorney did not accept representation.

Question 10.

A is the correct answer. A lawyer shall not form a partnership with a non-lawyer if any of the activities of the partnership consist of the "practice of law." A lawyer who does so is assisting another in the unauthorized practice of law, and is subject to discipline. Model Rule 5.5(a). Here, the important point is that the *partnership* is delivering the legal services, which choice A states explicitly.

B is incorrect. There is no absolute ban on lawyer and non-lawyer partnerships. As stated above, the issue is whether the partnership delivers legal services. For example, the attorney would not be subject to discipline if this partnership provided only accounting services.

C is incorrect. Again, the important fact is that the partnership is providing legal services. However, as a partner, the accountant is receiving a portion of the entity's profits and has control over the legal aspects of the business. Under Model Rule 5.4(a), a lawyer may not share legal fees with a non-lawyer, which would clearly happen here under the partnership agreement. This rule is the major deterrent to partnerships like this, and even splitting fees with a charity is not allowed. The only exceptions to this rule involve paying the estates of deceased attorneys or law firm retirement plans, neither of which apply here. Consequently, what the accountant actually does in terms of work is not important, because, as a partner in this partnership, she is still engaged in the unauthorized practice of law.

D is incorrect. As stated above, the main issues are the creation of a partnership that provides legal services and the sharing of fees with a non-lawyer. Simply keeping the accountant from interfering with the attorney's professional obligations is not enough.

Question 11.

B is the correct answer. As long as the client is fully informed, a lawyer and client may agree to limit the scope of the lawyer's representation so long as the limitation is reasonable under the circumstances. Model Rule 1.2(c). Although clients usually retain a lawyer to take care of all aspects of a particular matter, if the client affirmatively consents after consultation, the client can limit the scope of the representation to only one part of the claim. Consequently, it is clearly permissible under the Rules for the client and the lawyer to agree to a representation that only covers the grand jury proceeding.

A is incorrect. The important issues are whether the client is informed, agrees, and the limitation is reasonable. Whose idea it was is completely irrelevant. While a client will usually be the one to suggest a limit to the scope of representation, if it was the attorney's suggestion, the analysis would still be the same.

C is incorrect. Lawyers are not obligated to provide free legal services, and the limited representation here puts the client in a better position than if he were represented by no lawyer at all. When an attorney and a client agree to limit the scope of a representation, the client's ability to pay is most likely the cause.

D is incorrect. The fact a case is a criminal or civil matter is also irrelevant.

Question 12.

D is the correct answer. A lawyer shall not reveal any information relating to the representation of a client unless the client gives informed consent. Model Rule 1.6(a). This is probably the most important rule in the Model Rules of Professional Conduct. It is intended to promote candid communications between the client and attorney, so all the aspects of a particular legal problem become known and the lawyer can provide the most competent legal advice. Importantly, if a client knew the attorney could share his or her confidences to third parties, competent representation would become much more difficult, if not impossible, as the client would likely leave the lawyer in the dark on many important facts. Here, although the prior murders are not part of the present case, this information was obtained during the course of the attorney's representation, and consequently "relates" to that representation. Additionally, the prior murders would likely affect the attorney's strategy in the present case, specifically whether his client should plead guilty or testify at trial.

A is incorrect. Although there are several exceptions to the Model Rule 1.6's confidentiality requirement, none of the exceptions requires an attorney to disclose a client's past crimes of violence. Under the major exceptions to the Rule, a lawyer may reveal confidences to the extent necessary to prevent the client from committing a crime causing imminent death or substantial bodily injury (including a client's potential suicide), to the extent necessary to establish a claim or defense in a controversy between the lawyer and the client, or to the extent necessary to prevent or rectify financial harm caused by a crime or fraud involving the lawyer's services. Often, when testing this particular issue, the MPRE uses "as an officer of the court" in its "distracter" answer choices.

B is incorrect. Despite the fact the attorney is impeding the state's access to significant evidence, he still has an obligation to keep the client's information confidential. This answer option is trying to prey on your sympathies to the victims' families. Don't fall for the "sympathy" choice.

C is incorrect. As stated above, although the attorney did not advise the client with respect to the prior crimes, he discovered that information during his representation of the client during this matter. However, if the attorney had advised the client regarding how to commit the prior crimes or how to hide the bodies, he would be subject to discipline and criminal prosecution.

Question 13.

D is the correct answer. A lawyer who was formerly employed by a government agency may not later represent a client "in connection with a matter in which the lawyer participated personally and substantially" as a public employee, unless the government agency consents in writing. Model Rule 1.11(a)(2). If the lawyer is practicing in a firm, this disqualification would cover any other lawyer in the firm unless the firm puts together a screening arrangement and gives written notice to the agency. Model Rule 1.11(b). Here, the attorney participated personally and substantially by conducting a title search on the client's property when he was employed by the government agency. Furthermore, the attorney may not disclose the confidential information he learned while working at the department because a lawyer who was formerly employed by a government agency must not reveal confidential information relating to a former representation. Model Rules 1.11(a)(1) and 1.9(c).

A is incorrect. Because the attorney participated personally and substantially in the matter as a public employee, he cannot now represent the client unless the government agency consents in writing, whether or not he plans to use the confidential information he learned while working there. Importantly, even if he only represents the client on damages, he will still be representing her "in connection with a matter in which the lawyer participated personally and substantially."

B is incorrect. As stated above, he can neither represent the client nor disclose the confidential information.

C is incorrect. Whether or not he represents the client, he still cannot disclose the government's confidential information. Model Rules 1.11(a)(1) and 1.9(c).

Question 14.

D is the correct answer. These facts invoke the concepts of conflicts of interest and imputed disqualification. Model Rule 1.9 deals with the conflict faced by a lawyer who has represented one client, terminates the representation, and then is asked to represent a new client with interests adverse to those of the lawyer's former client. If you simplify these facts, it's clear that the former assistant district attorney could not himself represent the co-defendant after he participated in the investigation of the co-defendant because the interests of the co-defendant are adverse to the former assistant district attorney's interests. Model Rule 1.9(a). But the question asks about the attorney's representation of the co-defendant, not the former assistant district attorney's. Model Rule 1.10(a) extends the former assistant district attorney's disqualification to the attorney under the imputed disqualification rule: "While lawyers are associated in a firm, none of them shall knowingly represent a client when any one of them practicing alone would be prohibited from doing so by Model Rules 1.7. or 1.9."

A is incorrect. Model Rule 1.9 doesn't give the lawyer with the prohibited conflict the discretion to decide that he or she can protect the interests of the new client by protecting confidences. Under these circumstances, the lawyer may not represent the new client if (1) the lawyer himself or herself formerly represented a client in a substantially related matter with interests adverse to the new client's interests (Model Rule 1.9 (a)) or (2) the lawyer was associated with a firm representing a client with interests adverse to his or her present client, about whom the lawyer acquired information protected by the confidentiality rules that is material to the new client's matter (Model Rule 1.9(b)(2)).

B is incorrect. It states correctly a basic rule that prosecutors must follow, but it is not responsive to the question. The facts do not suggest that there was any exculpatory evidence, or that the former assistant district attorney knew of or withheld any. Also, the statement in B is irrelevant to the facts because the former assistant district attorney is no longer a prosecutor.

C is incorrect. The initial prohibition is directed at the former assistant district attorney because he's the lawyer with the conflict between the former and present clients. But the prohibition extends to the attorney under the imputed disqualification rule, whether or not the former assistant district attorney participates. Model Rule 1.10.

Question 15.

A is the correct answer. The question deals with the general obligation of a lawyer not to reveal any information relating to representation of a client without the client's consent after consultation. The obligation is defined in Model Rule 1.6(a). Model Rule 1.6(b) creates three exceptions to the general rule. One of the exceptions permits a lawyer to reveal a client confidence to defend him- or herself in a controversy with the client or against a criminal charge or civil claim for conduct involving the client, or to respond to allegations in any proceeding concerning the representation. Because the defendant has made a serious charge that would have grave consequences for the attorney if accepted as true, the attorney has a right to reveal the contents of the client's letter.

B is incorrect. Although the client has indeed committed a fraud on the court, the attorney would be obligated not to reveal the fraud except for the need to protect himself against the false accusation of complicity. General client fraud does not fall within one of the exceptions to the general duty of confidentiality.

C is incorrect. Whether or not the attorney learned the facts in confidences, he has a right to disclose them to protect himself in the disciplinary proceeding.

D is incorrect. When a lawyer is accused of a disciplinary infraction, he or she has a right to disclose a client's confidences to defend him- or herself. In the balance between the lawyer's right to defend himself or herself and the consequences to the client of revealing the client's confidence, the Rules have tipped the scales in favor of the lawyer, whose livelihood and reputation are at stake. Otherwise, the lawyer would be unable to defend himself or herself.

Question 16.

C is the correct answer. Under Model Rule 1.18, a prospective client is a person who discusses with the lawyer the possibility of forming a client-lawyer relationship with respect to a certain matter. The Comment to the Rule recognizes that prospective clients should receive some but not all of the protection afforded clients. Here, the attorney talked to the prospective client, declined the representation, gave the man another lawyer's name, and urged him to contact the other lawyer in a timely manner. Under the Rule, the attorney did not owe the prospective client any other duty, except that he must not mislead the prospective client into believing the attorney will represent him, and he must also protect any confidential information revealed by the prospective client. Model Rules 3.3 and 1.6.

A is incorrect because the attorney did not advertise falsely. The advertisement did not state, either expressly or impliedly, that he would take every case presented to him. Importantly, advertising in and of itself does not create an attorney-client relationship. False or misleading advertising is improper, but a lawyer may communicate that he or she practices certain types of law. Model Rules 7.1 and 7.4. However, with certain historical exceptions (such as "patent attorney"), a lawyer may not state or imply he or she is a specialist in a particular field of law unless the lawyer has been certified as a specialist by an organization that has been approved by an appropriate state authority or the American Bar Association. Model Rule 7.4. The name of any certifying organization must be clearly identified in the communication.

B is incorrect. Under these circumstances, the attorney was not required to give the man the exact date the statute of limitations would run. However, if that date had been within a very short time, such as one to two days instead of the six months here, the attorney may have had a duty to warn him.

D is incorrect. This answer implies that the reason the attorney is not subject to civil liability is because he offered to give the man a referral. However, as stated above, the reason the attorney is not subject to liability is because he did everything that was required under Model Rule 1.18. Always pick the answer that addresses the exact requirements and concerns of the particular Rule being tested.

Question 17.

C is the correct answer. A lawyer may not knowingly counsel or assist a client in conduct the lawyer knows is criminal or fraudulent. Model

Rule 1.2(d). When the client's course of action has already begun and is continuing, the lawyer is required to avoid assisting the client in the criminal act, such as by suggesting how the wrongdoing can be concealed. Here, although the client is engaged in continuing illegal conduct by remaining a fugitive, the attorney is not actually counseling or assisting the client in doing so (in fact, he encouraged the client to surrender). The important point in the Rule is "counsel or assist" in the criminal act. Consequently, the attorney is acting correctly under the Rules.

A is incorrect. While the client is engaging in continuing illegal conduct, the client is nevertheless entitled to the advice of a lawyer, and the attorney is not helping her to remain in hiding. Importantly, the attorney may discuss the legal consequences of any proposed course of conduct and may counsel or assist the client in making a good faith effort to determine the validity, scope, meaning, or application of the law. Model Rule 1.2(d).

B is incorrect. If a lawyer gives appropriate advice, he or she cannot be disciplined simply because his or her client refuses to listen.

D is incorrect. Whether or not the indictment is defective, the attorney is still acting appropriately here.

Question 18.

C is the correct answer. "In representing a client, a lawyer shall not communicate about the subject of the representation with a person the lawyer knows to be represented by another lawyer in the matter, unless the lawyer has the consent of the other lawyer or is authorized to do so by law or a court order." Model Rule 4.2. This Rule applies even though the represented person initiates or consents to the communication. Importantly, "a lawyer must immediately terminate communication with a person if, after commencing communication, the lawyer learns that the person is one with whom communication is not permitted by this Rule." Here, the attorney clearly violated this rule by negotiating with the owner.

A is incorrect. The represented person's lawyer is the one who must consent, not the represented person. Consequently, as stated above, Rule 4.2 applies even if the represented person initiates or consents to the communication.

B is incorrect. The prohibition is on any communication, and is not based on the signing of any documents.

D is incorrect. Under Rule 4.2, communication is prohibited only when the lawyer knows that the person is represented by another lawyer. This means that the lawyer must have actual knowledge of the representation, but such knowledge may be inferred from the circumstances. Thus, although the Rule imposes no duty on the lawyer to investigate, the lawyer cannot evade the Rule by ignoring the obvious.

Question 19.

D is the correct answer. The guiding rule is Model Rule 1.7, which deals with conflicts of interest. Unless the son is able to prove fraud and undue influence, you must assume that the client intended to cut his son's bequest in half. Thus, his son's position is directly adverse to the client's. If the client were still alive, Model Rule 1.7(a) would preclude representation of his son by the attorney because the interests of two clients would be directly adverse to each other. Now that the client is dead, the attorney is still constrained by Model Rule 1.7(a)(2), which also directs a lawyer not to represent a client if representation of that client may be materially limited by the lawyer's responsibilities to another client or to a third person. (A deceased client is still a client for purpose of this Rule.) Note also that the attorney will necessarily be called as witness to execution of the will and the behavior and circumstances of the deceased client. Because a lawyer may not act as advocate at a trial in which the lawyer is likely to be a necessary witness on a disputed issue (Model Rule 3.7), the attorney should not agree to represent the son in this will contest.

A is incorrect. The client's death does not trigger a release of the attorney from her duty of loyalty to the client. The second will is assumed to express the client's intent. The loyalty that the attorney owed to the client is transferred to the client's will, which the attorney prepared and witnessed.

B is incorrect. Although it correctly states one fact, that fact is immaterial to the issue raised by the entire fact pattern. The issue is the ability of a lawyer to represent two clients with directly adverse interests at the same time.

C is incorrect. First of all, it is incorrect on the law. A lawyer is not a guarantor of the validity of a will that he or she prepares. His or her job is to restate in legally sufficient form the intent of the testator and, if asked to do so, to supervise the proper execution of the will. Also, the statement is irrelevant to the issue raised by the facts.

Question 20.

C is the correct answer. The essence of our judicial system is the open and public development of facts and issues before jury and judge.

Consequently, neither lawyer may communicate with the judge or any juror who is not simultaneously or equally available to the other lawyer. The intent is to prevent undue influence by either side. Further, Model Rule 3.5(b) says specifically, "A lawyer shall not . . . communicate ex parte with such a person [judge, juror, prospective juror or other official] during the proceeding unless authorized to do so by law or court order." Here, however noble his intent, the attorney called the judge without advising his adversary that he would do. This was a direct violation of the rules.

A is incorrect. Ex parte contact with a judge is not permitted even if it ultimately leads to an argument by both sides. Obviously, an ex parte conversation between a lawyer and the judge is not monitored for content. Although it may lead to open argument, it's always possible that some nuance or some ingredient in the original conversation has already worked its influence on the judge.

B is incorrect for the same basic reason as A. Ex parte contacts with judge or jury are prohibited, period.

D is incorrect. Whether or not the ex parte contact leads to a better result, it is prohibited. If it were not, one could never be certain that the record of a trial correctly reflected the testimony or the arguments that influenced the outcome.

Question 21.

D is the correct answer. A lawyer is prohibited from knowingly making a false statement of material fact or law to a third person in the course of representing a client. Model Rule 4.1. Omissions that rise to the level of an affirmative false statement are also improper. Importantly, the Rule applies only to statements of *material fact.* Under generally accepted standards of negotiation, certain types of statements ordinarily are not taken as statements of material fact. Model Rule 4.1, Comment [2]. Estimates of price, value, or settlement maximums are ordinarily placed in this category, and are considered mere "puffing" on the part of the attorney. Here, the attorney's comments as to "steady profits" amounted to mere "puffing."

A is incorrect. Here, although the lawyer may have exaggerated the value of his client's business, this exaggeration would not be considered a statement of material fact for the reasons stated above.

B is incorrect. This answer choice is basically the same choice as A, except choice A is stating a suggested legal reason for discipline, while choice B is stating the factual way the attorney might be violating that legal reason

(that is, the attorney is making a false statement of fact by exagg‹
profitability of the business). Because only one answer choice
correct, recognizing the similarity between the two choices cancels out
both answer choices.

C is incorrect. Under Model Rule 4.1, it is irrelevant which party the
lawyer represents.

Question 22.

C is the correct answer. It is clear that a lawyer may advertise his or her
services. Under Model Rule 7.2, a lawyer may advertise by any public
medium or through written or recorded communication. The right is
subject, however, to Model Rules 7.1 and 7.3. Model Rule 7.1 imposes the
requirement that the advertisement not be false or misleading. Generally,
so long as the statements in the advertisement are truthful, the ad
passes muster. Model Rule 7.3 forbids direct solicitation either in person
or by telephone. Here, no part of the attorney's ad would seem to be
anything more than a statement of simple facts about the attorney.

A is incorrect. The advertisement need not state the lawyer's qualifications. On the contrary, a lawyer who ventures to state his or her qualifications risks the possibility that he or she will overstate them. Comment
[2] to Model Rule 7.2 lists some of the matters a lawyer may list with
impunity: name, address, telephone number, range of services, basis for
fees, foreign language ability, references and, with their consent, names of
clients regularly represented.

B is incorrect. Nothing in this ad can reasonably be construed as
encouraging litigation.

D is incorrect. Many radio and television stations can be heard across state
lines. As long as a lawyer licensed in one state does not state that he or
she is able to practice in a state in which he or she is not licensed, it
will be assumed that his or her ad is directed only at listeners and
viewers in the state in which he or she is licensed.

Question 23.

C is the correct answer. Under Model Rule 7.2, lawyers are permitted to
advertise, subject to Model Rule 7.1, which prohibits a lawyer from
making false or misleading statements about his or her services, and
Model Rule 7.3, which limits direct contact with prospective clients. So
long as there are no false or misleading statements in the attorney's
advertisement, he would not be subject to discipline for placing this ad.

A is incorrect. Option A refers to Model Rule 7.3(a), which prohibits a lawyer from making *an in-person or live telephone or real-time electronic contact* with a prospective client unless the lawyer has had a prior relationship with the prospective client. This question deals with written advertising.

B is incorrect. There is no reason the attorney shouldn't use a coupon in his advertisement.

D is incorrect. The issue here is whether the advertisement meets the requirements of the Rules. The attorney is placing a general written advertisement and has no way of knowing whether a person is currently represented by another lawyer.

Question 24.

D is the correct answer. Ordinarily, a lawyer is duty-bound to report another lawyer's violation of the Model Rules of Professional Conduct if the violation raises a substantial question as to that lawyer's honesty, trustworthiness, or fitness as a lawyer. Model Rule 8.3. However, when the information about the violation is protected under the client confidentiality rules of Model Rule 1.6, this duty becomes discretionary. Even so, Comment [2] to Model Rule 8.3 advises: "However, a lawyer should encourage a client to consent to disclosure where prosecution would not substantially prejudice the client's interests." On these facts, which show that the client would be reluctant to report the other attorney because he is an old friend, the attorney would probably be wasting her breath to encourage the disclosure of the other attorney's neglect of the client's interests. Ultimately, because the information about the violation is protected under client confidentiality rules (because the client told the attorney about the violation during the course of her representation of him), the attorney will not be subject to discipline if she chooses not to report the other attorney without the client's consent.

A is incorrect. Whether or not the attorney believes the other attorney was guilty of professional misconduct, she will not be subject to discipline if she chooses not to report the other attorney without the client's consent.

B is incorrect. If there is no Model Rule 1.6 confidentiality issue, the attorney's belief as to the other attorney's usual conduct would be immaterial. The duty to report another lawyer's misconduct of which a lawyer has knowledge is absolute, not discretionary. Once an act of misconduct is known, it becomes a matter for the "appropriate professional authority," not for the lawyer. Only when the client tells the lawyer in confidence and does not consent to disclosure can the lawyer choose not to report another attorney.

C is incorrect. The trigger that converts the attorney's duty from an absolute duty to a discretionary option is the lack of the client's consent, not the level of the client's satisfaction with the other attorney or the fact that the client was not out of money.

Question 25.

A is the correct answer. A lawyer must promptly notify the client on receiving funds, securities, or other properties in which the client has an interest. Model Rule 1.15(d). In addition, except as otherwise permitted by law or by agreement with the client, a lawyer shall promptly deliver to the client any funds or property the client is entitled to receive and, on request by the client, promptly render a full accounting regarding such property. Here, the attorney deliberately delayed notifying the client for a week so the client could take investing classes. The fact that the attorney was arguably doing so in the client's best interest is irrelevant.

B is incorrect. The lawyer was permitted to give this unsolicited advice. Under Model Rule 2.1, a lawyer who is advising a client "shall exercise independent professional judgment and render candid advice." In doing so, the lawyer may "refer not only to law but to other considerations such as moral, economic, social, and political factors that may be relevant to the client's situation."

C is incorrect. The lawyer's failure to promptly notify the client of the lawyer's receipt of the client funds is not excused by the client's later failure to object. Many times, the MPRE will try to conceal a wrong answer by having the client later consent to the attorney's violation of the Rules.

D is incorrect. Under Rule 1.15(d), as stated above, there is no exception when the lawyer thinks it would be in the client's best interest to delay notification.

Question 26.

C is the correct answer. Even though this is a somewhat limited communication, it is clearly an advertisement for the attorney's new law office, and as such is covered by Model Rule 7.1. Model Rule 7.1 forbids only false or misleading communications, and this communication was neither false nor misleading. Here, all the communication did was state the simple facts regarding the reopening of the office, its location and phone number, and the fact that the attorney had been the state's governor for eight years.

A is incorrect. A lawyer is prohibited from making in-person, live telephone, or real-time electronic contact with prospective clients to solicit employment when the lawyer's motive for doing so is the lawyer's financial gain. Model Rule 7.3(a). This Rule seeks to address the fact that "the prospective client, who may already feel overwhelmed by the circumstances giving rise to the need for legal services, may find it difficult to fully evaluate all available alternatives with reasoned judgment and appropriate self-interest in the face of the lawyer's presence and insistence upon being retained immediately." Model Rule 7.3, Comment [1]. However, there is an exception for contacts with former clients, friends, other lawyers, or relatives, which is what this answer choice is trying to get you to think of, since this communication is only going out to those people who fall within this exception. However, as the communication here is simply a printed announcement, it does not fall within this type of banned behavior, so the exception does not apply.

B is incorrect. Model Rule 7.1 forbids only false or misleading communications in lawyer advertising. However, an advertisement can be misleading if it creates an unjustified expectation as to the results the lawyer may achieve. Here, a truthful statement about the attorney's prior service as governor is unlikely to create any unjustified expectations as to what the attorney can achieve and is therefore not misleading.

D is incorrect. Depending on how it is used in the advertisement, information in the public domain can still be either false or misleading.

Question 27.

D is the correct answer. In construing the propriety of a lawyer's contribution in a judicial election campaign, the ABA Model Rules and the ABA Model Code of Judicial Conduct must be read in tandem. Model Rule 3.5(a) prohibits a lawyer from seeking to influence a judge or juror. Although the other attorney is not a judge yet, he soon could be. Comment [1] to Model Rule 3.5 says: "Many forms of improper influence upon a tribunal [. . .] are specified in the ABA Model Code of Judicial Conduct, with which an advocate should be familiar." The cases and the disciplinary rulings in all states almost invariably construe a loan or gift to a judge by a lawyer who appears before him or her as an attempt to influence the judge. Thus, a contribution to the other attorney's campaign may not be made by a gift to the other attorney personally under Model Rule 3.5. Further, Rule 4.1(A)(8) of the Model Code of Judicial Conduct states, a candidate shall not "personally solicit or accept campaign contributions other than through a campaign committee authorized by Rule 4.4." D correctly recognizes that the attorney may make his contribution to the other attorney's campaign committee.

A is incorrect. The attorney may not give the contribution to the other attorney personally. The underlying reason for the rule prohibiting giving personal gifts directly to the candidate is that it will lead to excessive influence by the donor lawyer when he or she appears before that person if that person in fact becomes a judge.

B is incorrect. The rules do not require that the gift be made anonymously, only that it not be made to the person running for judge personally. A donation to the judge's duly constituted campaign committee is perfectly proper.

C is incorrect. A lawyer may contribute to a judge's campaign committee whether or not he or she appears before the judge. This recognizes the fact that lawyers who appear before a judge are better able than others to determine whether the judge is really qualified.

Question 28.

B is the correct answer. "A lawyer shall not make a statement that the lawyer knows to be false or with reckless disregard as to its truth or falsity concerning the qualifications or integrity of a judge, adjudicatory officer, or public legal officer, or of a candidate for election or appointment to judicial or legal office." Model Rule 8.2(a). However, lawyers' assessments are necessarily relied on in determining the fitness of persons being considered for election or appointment to judicial offices. Model Rule 8.2, Comment [1]. Consequently, the attorney's expression of good faith views about a judicial candidate's qualifications was proper, because "[e]xpressing honest and candid opinions on such matters contributes to improving the administration of justice." Model Rule 8.2, Comment 1. The Rule targets false statements, not honest opinions.

A is incorrect. Even if the attorney was seeking judicial office, it was still proper for him to provide good-faith opinions about the judicial candidate's qualifications because such opinions promote the administration of justice by assisting the voters in making informed electoral decisions. Model Rule 8.2, Comment [1]. If he were a candidate for public office, the attorney would be required to comply with the applicable provisions of the Model Code of Judicial Conduct. Model Rule 8.2(b). However, the Model Code does not forbid comments such as those made by the attorney.

C is incorrect. Although false statements about judicial candidates can unfairly undermine public confidence in the administration of justice, a lawyer's good-faith expressions of opinion about a judicial candidate's temperament, based on the lawyer's experience, promotes the administration of justice by helping voters make informed decisions. Model Rule 8.2. Also, the lawyer running for election has not yet served in the judiciary, so any comments regarding his ability and temperament would say nothing regarding the judiciary.

D is incorrect. As stated above, although false public statements about a judicial candidate's qualifications are improper, lawyers are entitled to make truthful public statements about judicial candidates.

Question 29.

B is the correct answer. Model Rule 1.3 states: "An attorney shall act with reasonable diligence and promptness in representing a client." Comment [2] states: ". . . A lawyer's work load must be controlled so that each matter can be handled competently." Comment [3] states: "Perhaps no professional shortcoming is more widely resented than procrastination . . . when a lawyer overlooks a statute of limitations, the client's legal position may be destroyed. Even when a client's interests are not affected in substance, however, unreasonable delay can cause a client needless anxiety and undermine confidence in the lawyer's trustworthiness." The facts here show the typical way a lawyer can end up subject to discipline: (1) make appointments and ignore them, (2) ignore the client's phone calls and requests for information and progress reports, (3) fail to keep the client advised, (4) work on other matters to the exclusion or neglect of the client, and (5) ignore the passage of time and the inevitable running of the statute of limitations. The key word in Answer B is "neglect." Here, the attorney has been guilty of professional neglect. After misuse of client funds, this is the most common basis for lawyer discipline.

A is incorrect. Commitment to one or several clients to the neglect of another is exactly what Model Rule 1.3 was intended to prevent.

C is incorrect. The attorney is not relieved of the consequences of her neglect because the passenger avoided the running of the statute. The passenger has already suffered in other ways. First, if the attorney had pursued her settlement negotiations, the passenger might have enjoyed the proceeds of settlement many months earlier. Second, the attitude of the bus company may have hardened in the interim and made settlement more difficult. Third, the passenger could have been spared the anguish and frustration caused by unanswered phone calls and worry about her claim.

D is incorrect. The issue is not the retainer, but rather the attorney's neglect of the passenger's interests.

Question 30.

C is the correct answer. Model Rule 3.2 directs a lawyer to make reasonable efforts to expedite litigation consistent with the interests of the client. Model Rule 1.3 directs a lawyer to act with reasonable diligence and promptness in representing a client. Model Rule 3.4 covers fairness to opposing counsel, specifically issues such as falsifying evidence and inducing witnesses to give false testimony. Even though the attorney knows the insurance company is represented by another attorney, nothing in Model Rule 3.4 states that the attorney must warn the opposing attorney of a possible default judgment. Importantly, such a requirement could force a lawyer to violate Model Rules 3.2 and 1.3.

A is incorrect. For the same reasons as above, the attorney's knowledge that another attorney represented the insurance company did not give the attorney an obligation to inform the other attorney of the default judgment.

B is incorrect. If the attorney knew the other attorney and had dealt with him in other matters, it might have been preferable to advise the other attorney before entering the default in order to avoid the other attorney's anger, but nothing required the attorney to do so.

D is incorrect. First, this answer choice is not responsive to the question. Second, each step in a litigation requires prompt action by a lawyer. Whether or not the insurance company will pay, the attorney must protect her client's interests at every step.

Question 31.

C is the correct answer. Candidates for judicial office must observe the provisions of the Model Code of Judicial Conduct governing judicial campaigns and elections. Most of these provisions are contained in Canon 4. Rule 4.1(A)(11) provides that a candidate shall not "knowingly or with reckless disregard for the truth, make any false or misleading statement." Importantly, a person's knowledge may be inferred from the circumstances. Here, the attorney does not have actual knowledge that the judge was not reprimanded for misconduct in office. Nor was it unreasonable for her to rely on the statement of an official directly responsible for maintaining the information at issue.

A is incorrect. It assumes that the attorney had a duty to inquire into the records themselves after getting a response to her inquiry from the director of the commission himself. This was not a reasonable requirement to impose on the attorney.

B is incorrect. The test is not the truth of the statement but whether the attorney has knowledge of the truth.

D is incorrect. The answer suggests that judges are held to a different standard in contested elections than in non-contested elections. However, even in a contested judicial election, there are constraints on the candidates that do not apply to candidates for non-judicial offices. See Canon 4.

Question 32.

B is the correct answer. Lawyers are officers of the court and are charged with the responsibility not to make statements with reckless disregard for the truth concerning the qualifications or integrity of a judge. Model Rule 8.2. Comment [1] points out that false statements by a lawyer can undermine public confidence in the administration of justice. Here, the attorney has attacked the integrity not only of one judge, but of the entire judiciary. Especially because his work as a skilled litigator brings him before these very judges, who decide both fact and law, the inescapable inference is that he has special influence over them.

A is incorrect. A lawyer may contribute to a judge's campaign committee without accounting for his or her motivation in doing so. The Model Code of Judicial Conduct permits the campaign committees of judges to solicit funds from lawyers, but the funds may not be used for the private benefit of the candidates.

C is incorrect. If the statements are indeed true, then the attorney is subject to discipline under Model Rule 3.5 for seeking "to influence a judge, juror, prospective juror or other official by means prohibited by law."

D is incorrect. It's immaterial to the attorney's misconduct that the prospective client did not retain him.

Question 33.

D is the correct answer. Each side is entitled to know and to respond to every fact and every argument presented by the other side. If a judge could consult any legal source he or she wished without identifying it and giving each side the right to respond, the adversarial nature of the judicial system would collapse. At the same time, there are instances in which a judge will need to get advice on the law, especially when, as in these facts, the lawyers have not cleared up all the issues. To enable the judge to do this without subverting the adversarial process, Model Code of Judicial

Conduct, Rule 2.9(A)(2) permits a judge to "obtain the written advice of a disinterested expert on the law applicable to a proceeding before the judge, if the judge gives advance notice to the parties of the person to be consulted and the subject matter of the advice to be solicited, and affords the parties a reasonable opportunity to object and respond to the notice and to the advice received."

A is incorrect. It's not enough that the expert consulted by the judge be impartial. The parties are entitled to know what the expert has been asked and what he or she has advised. After all, the expert may be wrong or the judge may not have communicated the issues correctly. The parties may want to respond, and they must be given the opportunity to do so.

B is incorrect. What's at issue here is not the judge's integrity, but the very process by which adversarial issues are determined under the judicial process.

C is incorrect only because it doesn't correspond with how the Model Code of Judicial Conduct resolves this issue. Under the Model Code, it is possible for the judge to ask for advice so long as he or she tells the parties what he or she is doing and gives them the opportunity to respond.

Question 34.

C is the correct answer. "In making administrative appointments, a judge: (1) shall exercise the power of appointment impartially and on the basis of merit; and (2) shall avoid nepotism, favoritism, and unnecessary appointments." Model Code of Judicial Conduct, Rule 2.13(A)(2). Here, the judge is violating the Rule by unnecessarily appointing special masters regardless of the nature and complexity of a proceeding. Additionally, the underlying theme of the Model Code of Judicial Conduct is to avoid creating the *appearance* of impropriety. Here, the decision of the judge to appoint special masters without reference to need arguably creates such an appearance.

A is incorrect. Achieving competence and impartiality does not justify making special master appointments in all cases before a judge. As stated above, the important point is that the judge must avoid making unnecessary appointments.

B is incorrect. Even if a special master charges a reasonable rate, the judge is still violating the rule by making unnecessary appointments.

D is incorrect. Nothing in the Model Code prohibits a judge from using a law directory to make appointments. In fact, using general law directories in compiling the list is a logical way for the judge to avoid the appearance of either nepotism or favoritism.

Question 35.

B is the correct answer. Because the attorney is newly admitted, he may not realize that he's become party to a scheme that enables the trust company to engage in the unauthorized practice of law. Model Rule 5.5(a) says quite simply, "A lawyer shall not practice law in a jurisdiction in violation of the regulation of the legal profession in that jurisdiction, or assist another in doing so." The attorney is enabling the trust company to discuss and "work out" the details of trusts and wills, functions that clearly fall within the parameters of law practice. The attorney is also aiding the trust company and its officer to misrepresent to the customer the way in which the documents are being prepared. The arrangement between the attorney and the trust company is in the nature of a partnership, and Model Rule 5.4(b) prevents a lawyer from forming a partnership with a non-lawyer if the function of the partnership is the practice of law. Also, even if the attorney is not sharing in the trust company's fees directly, he is in effect doing so by getting free office space. Importantly, Model Rule 5.4(a) prohibits fee splitting with non-lawyers. Ultimately, the attorney is subject to discipline for his actions.

A is incorrect. Don't be confused by the phrase "restricting the right to practice." It may suggest to you the restrictions against a lawyer's right to practice that are contained in Model Rule 5.6. But Model Rule 5.6 deals with restrictions imposed by restrictive employment agreements between a lawyer and his or her partners or law firm and by settlement agreements resolving controversies between private parties. Except for these provisions, which are intended to prevent economic pressure on a lawyer either to gain or keep employment or to settle a pending matter, there are no rules preventing a lawyer from restricting the range or extent of his or her practice.

C is incorrect. A lawyer is not required to charge a client for his or her services. The problem here is not the failure to charge, but the fact that the attorney is helping the trust company engage in the unauthorized practice of law.

D is incorrect. The important point is that the attorney is participating in an arrangement that enables persons who are not authorized to practice law to give legal advice.

Question 36.

C is the correct answer. Here, the attorney has represented both husband and wife in a business transaction, and then in resolving a business dispute between them. Each is a former client. As such, each is entitled to the protective umbrella of Model Rule 1.9. Model Rule 1.9(a) states that a lawyer who has formerly represented a client in a matter shall not thereafter represent another person in the same or a substantially related matter in which that person's interests are materially adverse to the interests of the former client, unless the former client consents after consultation. Further, a lawyer who has formerly represented a client in a matter may not use information relating to the former representation to the disadvantage of the former client (with exceptions not relevant here). Model Rule 1.9(c)(1). Under these facts, the attorney may not represent the wife in litigation against her husband.

A is incorrect. The important point is that the attorney represented both parties in the past, not that the husband may have lied to the attorney as well.

B is incorrect. The rule against representing a current client in an action adverse to the interests of a former client protects all former clients, whatever the facts.

D is incorrect. Again, Model Rule 1.9 is designed to protect a former client against an adverse action on behalf of a current or prospective client. That the former client is now represented by new counsel is irrelevant to the application of the rule.

Question 37.

B is the correct answer. Subject to prior limitations on the scope of representation and the lawyer's duty not to assist a client in criminal conduct, a lawyer "shall abide by a client's decisions concerning the objectives of representation." Model Rule 1.2(a). Specifically, a lawyer must abide by a client's decision to settle a matter, or, in a criminal case, the client's decision as to the "plea to be entered, whether to waive jury trial, and whether the client will testify." Model Rule 1.2(a). However, the lawyer has implied authorization to decide what actions are required to achieve the client's goals, as long as the lawyer consults with the client. Model Rule 1.4(a)(2). Here, once the client decided to settle, the attorney was required to accept the offer, whether or not the attorney reasonably believed the appeal was filed to gain an advantage in the settlement negotiations.

A is incorrect. Although the percentage increase gives the attorney an incentive to favor going through the appeal, this incentive does not create an impermissible conflict of interest. The important point in this question is that the client directed the attorney to settle.

C is incorrect. As stated above, the client makes any decision regarding settlement. A settlement is an objective of representation. Tactical matters are things such as the extent of discovery and what witnesses will be presented at trial.

D is incorrect. Although it is true that evaluating the merits of an appeal requires the exercise of independent professional judgment, this does not change the fact that the client has the ultimate authority in deciding whether to settle a matter.

Question 38.

A is the correct answer. A lawyer may advertise his or her services in the same media as any other professional or merchant. Model Rule 7.2. There are, however, special limitations that apply only to lawyers. The most important is embodied in Model Rule 7.1. Model Rule 7.1 requires that the lawyer not make a misleading statement about himself or herself or his or her services. A statement is misleading if it contains a material misrepresentation of fact or law, omits a fact that will make the statement not misleading, is likely to create unjustified expectations about the results the lawyer is likely to achieve, or compares the lawyer's services with other lawyers' services without substantiation in fact. Here, the ad televised by the attorney meets all of these requirements on its face. Even the last sentence is not objectionable. It suggests only that the attorney may have a relatively low fee schedule, or that potential clients may have a mistaken notion about the level of legal fees in the attorney's area. Also, the attorney is complying with the requirement to maintain copies of all of her ads.

B is incorrect. The ad does not state that the attorney's fees are lower than those generally charged in her area, only that the potential client may have a mistaken notion about legal fees in general. Further, a statement that the attorney's fees were lower than those generally charged in her area would not be improper if the statement could be supported by the facts.

C is incorrect. Nothing in the Rules prevents a lawyer from using professional actors to read a radio or TV ad. The actor is obviously not pretending to be the attorney; he is simply conveying her message in the same way as in other TV ads. If a lawyer did instruct an actor to pretend to be the lawyer when reading the ad, that, of course, would represent a material misrepresentation of fact and could lead to discipline.

D is incorrect. Nothing in the Rules prohibits a lawyer from charging for an initial consultation and nothing in the ad suggests that the attorney will not charge for the consultation.

Question 39.

B is the correct answer. Although Model Rule 1.6 protects a client's confidential information under the attorney-client privilege, one of the exceptions is that "a lawyer may reveal information relating to the representation of a client to the extent the lawyer reasonably believes necessary . . . to comply with other law or a court order." Model Rule 1.6(b)(6). However, "absent informed consent of the client to do otherwise, the lawyer should assert on behalf of the client all non-frivolous claims that the order is not authorized by other law or that the information sought is protected against disclosure by the attorney-client privilege." Model Rule 1.6, Comment [13]. In this case, the attorney has been subpoenaed to testify before a grand jury. Importantly, the clients' names may be confidential under Rule 1.6, but they are not protected by the attorney-client privilege. The attorney-client privilege protects only confidential communications between a lawyer and a client. It does not protect clients' identities unless disclosing their identities will implicitly reveal their confidential communications, which does not appear to be the case here. Thus, the attorney may provide the grand jury with the clients' names.

A is incorrect. Because the information isn't protected by the attorney-client privilege, it is irrelevant that negotiating a counterfeit bill is a crime.

C is incorrect. As stated above, the information is not confidential under Model Rule 1.6, so it is irrelevant whether it would fall under the exception that allows the disclosure of confidences to prevent imminent death or substantial bodily harm.

D is incorrect. As stated above, the information in this case is not privileged. However, if the attorney's information in this case were in fact privileged, it is true that the attorney could not disclose it under the "crime-fraud" exception, even though passing counterfeit money is a crime, because the attorney does not know which client paid with counterfeit bills, and also does not know whether the client who did so was aware the bills were counterfeit. Thus, if the attorney were to reveal confidential information, the attorney would be violating the Rule as to at least one innocent client who does not fall under the exception.

Question 40.

A is the correct answer. Under Model Rule 1.7(a), a lawyer shall not represent a client if the representation of one client will be directly adverse to the representation of another client. Here, the attorney has a conflict of interest arising from the representation of two clients in the same transaction — the bank, which is the lender, and the corporation, which is the borrower. However, Model Rule 1.7(b) allows the attorney to represent both clients if he reasonably believe that he will be able to provide competent and diligent representation to each client, the representation is not prohibited by law, the representation does not involve the assertion of a claim by one client against the other, and each client gives informed consent in writing. Here, because the proposed representation meets all the requirements of Model Rule 1.7(b), the joint representation is proper.

B is incorrect. Because the attorney has a conflict of interest under Model Rule 1.7(a), the fact that the arrangement is customary in the community is irrelevant. The important question is whether the proposed representation meets the requirements of Model Rule 1.7(b).

C is incorrect. "A lawyer shall not accept compensation for representing a client from other than the client unless: (1) the client gives informed consent; (2) there is no interference with the lawyer's independence of professional judgment or with the client-lawyer relationship; and (3) information relating to representation of a client is protected as required by Rule 1.6." Model Rule 1.8(f). The Rule recognizes the fact that third-party payers frequently have interests that differ from the client, such as minimizing the amount spent on the representation. The classic example of an arrangement violating this Rule is when a defendant's insurance company is responsible for the ultimate damage claim and is also paying the defendant's legal defense expenses. Here, in a joint representation such as this one, there is no restriction against the payment of legal fees by one of the two clients with informed consent. Model Rule 1.8(f).

D is incorrect. Although there is a conflict of interest, the attorney can represent clients with differing interests as long as the requirements of Model Rule 1.7(b) are met.

Question 41.

A is the correct answer. A lawyer may not counsel or assist a client in conduct that is criminal or fraudulent. Model Rule 1.2(d). Similarly, a lawyer has a duty under Model Rule 3.3(a)(3) not to use false evidence. When the attorney asked the client for his name, he knew that the response would be a falsehood that would mislead the court in its judgment of the client's offense.

B is incorrect. It's immaterial to the attorney's duty to the court whether the client committed a felony or a lesser crime. The point is the testimony would mislead the court into administering a lighter sentence than the law required.

C is incorrect. While the information would ordinarily be protected because it was disclosed to the attorney as a confidence during the course of representation, it cannot be protected if it results in the presentation of testimony that the attorney knows is false.

D is incorrect. The client's name is an issue in the trial. If the client's true name is used, he's subject to the heavier penalty. If the court doesn't learn his true name, the client gets the lighter penalty.

Question 42.

A is the correct answer. If a judge personally or as a fiduciary (trustee of a trust) has more than a de minimis economic interest in the subject matter in controversy, disqualification is required. Model Code of Judicial Conduct, Rule 2.11(A)(3). A financial interest disqualification can be remitted if the judge fully discloses the potential impartiality conflict on the record, all the parties and lawyers agree that the conflict is immaterial in a pro-ceeding outside the presence of the judge, and the agreement is then incorporated into the record. Model Code of Judicial Conduct, Rule 2.11(C). However, considering the large size of the financial interest ($50,000,000), a remittance here is likely inappropriate. Also, the potential for remittance was not included among any of the answer choices, making A the best answer.

B is incorrect. Even if the value of the stock is unlikely to be affected, disqualification is still necessary to prevent the appearance of judicial impropriety and the judge's impartiality can reasonably be questioned under the circumstances. The overarching goal of the Model Code of Judicial Conduct is to make sure judges act in a manner that promotes public confidence in the integrity, fairness, and impartiality of the judiciary. Consequently, members of the judiciary must avoid creating even an appearance of bias.

C is incorrect. Even if the judge does not personally own stock in either party to the litigation, she is a trustee who owns a legal interest in the stock while acting as a fiduciary for others with an equitable interest. Under these circumstances, the judge's impartiality can still be reasonably questioned by others. Further adding to the appearance of impropriety, the trust is set up for the educational benefit of the judge's grandchildren, and disqualification is similarly required in circumstances where a member of the judge's family has an economic interest in the matter.

D is incorrect. Although the judge believes she can be fair and impartial (and she might, in fact, be correct in this belief), that impartiality could be reasonably questioned by others. Consequently, she should disqualify herself for the same reasons as in B.

Question 43.

A is the correct answer. A judge's extra-judicial activities are always subject to scrutiny to "minimize the risk of conflict with judicial obligations." Model Code of Judicial Conduct, Canon 3. Rule 3.7(A) permits a judge to serve as an officer, director, trustee, or non-legal advisor of "educational, religious, charitable, fraternal, or civic organizations not conducted for profit . . ." (Note that the judge is precluded from giving any legal advice to the organization.) But the judge may not serve an organization that is engaged in a proceeding that is likely to come before the judge or that is engaged frequently in adversarial proceedings in the court of which the judge is a member. Rule 3.7(A)(6). Rule 3.13 permits a judge to accept "gifts incident to a public testimonial." However, there are limitations on testimonials. Importantly, the gift must not be one that would "appear to a reasonable person to undermine the judge's independence, integrity, or impartiality." Rule 3.13(A). On these facts, the judge may accept the portrait.

B is incorrect. The fact that the judge did not receive compensation is only one piece of the puzzle. Other pieces are also required to make the gift proper: (a) that it is a public testimonial, (b) by a charitable organization, (c) that does not engage in litigation before the judge's court. (Note: a judge may receive compensation for activities permitted under Canon 3 if the source of payment does not give the appearance of influencing the judge in his or her judicial duties and if the compensation is reasonable and does not exceed what a non-judge would receive for the same activity. Rule 3.12.)

C is incorrect. There is no specific limit in the Model Code for the cost of a testimonial gift. The test is whether the value of the gift is so excessive as to suggest undue influence either in a specific matter or generally, and, also, whether the source of the gift is suspect. (On this issue, see the next paragraph.)

D is incorrect. A testimonial gift from lawyers to a judge is not prohibited per se.

Question 44.

C is the correct answer. A lawyer in litigation is expected to be a zealous advocate of his or her client's position. If he or she is called to testify on a contested issue of fact, his or her role as advocate becomes confused. Also, his or her testimony may create an irreconcilable conflict of interest between the client and the attorney. For these reasons, a lawyer is prohibited from acting as advocate in a matter if he or she is likely to be called as a witness. Model Rule 3.7. However, there are three exceptions: (1) if the testimony relates to an uncontested issue, (2) if the testimony relates to the nature and value of the lawyer's services in the matter, or (3) if the lawyer's disqualification would cause substantial hardship to the client. Model Rule 3.7. Because the facts here do not present an exception to the general rule, the attorney may not represent the executor. The executor may retain other counsel and the attorney will then be free to testify about the client's competence. This question illustrates why a lawyer should never act as subscribing witness to a will he or she prepares. When a lawyer prepares a will and then acts as subscribing witness, he or she knows that he or she may later be called to appear as a witness in a contest of the will.

A is incorrect. It restates the problem, not the solution. It's exactly because the attorney is likely to be called as a witness that he may not represent the executor. True, there is some hardship on the executor in forcing him to find and retain other counsel to prove the will, but the problem is not insurmountable. On balance, the need to forestall participation by the lawyer as both advocate and witness is paramount.

B is incorrect. The rule against the lawyer as witness assumes that the lawyer would testify in support of his or her client. "The problem can arise whether the lawyer is called as a witness on behalf of his client or is called by the opposing party." Model Rule 3.7, Comment [6].

D is incorrect. It states correctly the underlying rationale for the rule, but not the rule itself. Whether or not the attorney's testimony supports one side or another, he may not represent either side if he is likely to be called as a necessary witness.

Question 45.

A is the correct answer. In settling a claim or potential claim for malpractice, a lawyer must advise an unrepresented client in writing of the desirability of seeking independent legal counsel. Model Rule 1.8(h)(2).

B is incorrect. The attorney's belief, or even whether the agreement is fair or unfair to the buyer, is not the issue. In this situation, under the Rules, the lawyer must advise the client in writing of the appropriateness of independent representation and must give the client ample time to find and consult with another lawyer.

C is incorrect. There is no prohibition on settling a potential malpractice claim, whether or not a related matter is ongoing.

D is incorrect. The Rules do not require that the buyer actually be separately represented, only that he be advised in writing of the desirability of seeking independent legal counsel and given time to consult with another lawyer.

Question 46.

A is the correct answer. If a lawyer identifies criminal behavior on the part of an opposing party, upon consent of the client, the lawyer may disclose such information to the prosecutor. Once the lawyer has the client's consent, disclosure of the information would be permissive, not mandatory.

B is incorrect. As stated above, the lawyer is not required to report an opposing party's criminal activity to the prosecutor. Additionally, the decision to report the defendant to the criminal authorities does not depend on whether the information discovered is privileged or not.

C is incorrect. There is no duty to inform the defendant's lawyer before reporting the information.

D is incorrect. It was permissible to report even though the civil suit was pending because the attorney was not trying to gain an advantage by making a complaint to the prosecutor. Had she been seeking an advantage, it might have been impermissible under Model Rule 3.4, which covers fairness to opposing party and counsel.

Question 47.

D is the correct answer. In making decisions and exercising options, a lawyer is required to act with competence. Model Rule 1.1. This means that he or she must employ "the legal knowledge, skill, thoroughness and preparation reasonably necessary for the representation." In other words, the lawyer is not a guarantor of a successful outcome or even of a consequence-free result. He or she is required, however, to exercise his or her judgment in a manner that would be considered reasonable by other lawyers under all the circumstances. There are circumstances in which a lawyer may reasonably advise a client not to respond to questions by a legislative fact-finding committee, even when the client is faced by the risk of imprisonment. These facts do not tell us what the underlying facts were, but they do state clearly that the attorney "reasonably believed" that it was in the best interests of the witness not to answer. Ultimately, the attorney is not subject to discipline so long as he acted reasonably.

A is incorrect. Whether or not the attorney ultimately made the right decision, he cannot be disciplined because he acted on a reasonable belief that he was protecting the witness. There is no suggestion in the facts that the attorney was not competent to represent the witness before the committee or to exercise his reasonable discretion to advise the witness not to answer.

B is incorrect. The facts do not disclose the constitutional basis for the refusal by the witness to answer the committee's questions. Obviously, however, the consequences to the witness in failing to exercise her constitutional rights were deemed by the attorney to be more serious and severe than the refusal to answer. Although the general rule is that an attorney may not counsel a client to engage, or assist a client, in conduct that the lawyer knows is criminal (Model Rule 1.2), most courts would support the witness' right to refuse to answer if her constitutional rights were in jeopardy.

C is incorrect. Model Rule 1.2 does not distinguish between crimes involving moral turpitude and other crimes. A lawyer may not assist a client in any crime, however characterized. However, the conflict between the need to protect a constitutional right not to answer and the obligation to observe a law requiring an answer is irreconcilable. The lawyer's obligation under these circumstances is to advise the client of the consequences of each alternative.

Question 48.

A is the correct answer. A newly admitted lawyer in a firm must have his or her work properly supervised by a more experienced lawyer to ensure that all lawyers in the firm conform to the Model Rules of Professional Conduct. Model Rule 5.1. Under Model Rule 1.1, a law firm owes a client a duty of competence, specifically the appropriate "legal knowledge, skill, thoroughness, and preparation necessary to the representation." Consequently, when a firm uses less-experienced lawyers to perform client work, the partners must supervise that work. In this case, the associate, who had never conducted or observed a trial and had not worked on landlord-tenant cases before, needed supervision. There was not enough time for the associate to become familiar with the relevant law and procedure, nor did she have the experience to competently handle the case. Importantly, the attorney did not take the proper precautions to make sure that the associate was adequately prepared to carry out the assignment.

B is incorrect. The outcome of the trial is irrelevant to whether the associate was properly supervised. In particular, be wary of answer choices where a good outcome "fixes" the violation.

C is incorrect. The associate's admission to the bar did not relieve the attorney of the responsibility to properly supervise and train her. The question of a lawyer's competence revolves around that lawyer's training and experience, not the simple fact that the lawyer has passed a bar exam.

D is incorrect. The consent of the landlord to this representation would not mitigate the fact that the attorney failed to properly supervise the associate. Also be wary of answer choices where a client consents to the Rule violation.

Question 49.

C is the correct answer. There is definitely a conflict of interest involved if the attorney represents the builder and the neighbor. A lawyer may not represent one client if it will be directly adverse to another client without the client's informed consent. Model Rule 1.7. This is true even if the lawyer would be acting as advocate against the client in a matter unrelated to the one in which the lawyer represents the client. Model Rule 1.7, Comment [6]. It is possible the attorney could undertake the representation of the neighbor with informed written consent from the builder, but since that option is not offered, C remains the best answer.

A is incorrect. The conflict of interest rule speaks to a lawyer's loyalty to a client, so it doesn't matter whether there are common issues in the two matters. If the attorney represents the neighbor in opposing the builder's petition for rezoning, the builder would likely feel betrayed, which would likely damage the attorney's and the builder's lawyer-client relationship and interfere with the attorney's representation of the builder in the contract suit.

B is incorrect for the same reasons that A is incorrect. Loyalty to the client is the issue, and again, it doesn't matter what types of proceedings are involved.

D is incorrect. The issue is dealing with a concurrent conflict; what might or might not happen in the future has nothing to do with the attorney's decision whether it is proper to undertake representation of the neighbor.

Question 50.

A is the correct answer. With regard to *civil cases,* the adversary system contemplates that the evidence in a case is to be marshaled competitively by the parties. Model Rule 3.4, Comment [1]. Likewise, a lawyer's duty not to conceal evidence in a civil case does not carry with it a duty to report or volunteer all relevant information. Prosecutors, however, have special responsibilities. Model Rule 3.8. "A prosecutor has the responsibility of a minister of justice and not simply that of an advocate" (Model Rule 3.8, Comment [1]) and as such, "must make timely disclosure to the defense of all evidence or information known to the prosecutor that tends to negate the guilt of accused . . ." Model Rule 3.8(d). The fact that the girls' descriptions varied significantly at one point, but later matched almost perfectly, raises a definite question as to the accuracy of their identification and "tends to negate the guilt" of the suspect. Here, the prosecutor has a duty to reveal the existence of the tape to the suspect's counsel.

B is incorrect. What the prosecutor believes is not the point. If there is evidence or information that would raise a question as to the guilt of the suspect, the prosecutor must disclose the existence of that information or evidence in a timely manner.

C is incorrect. This is a true statement with regard to civil cases. See Model Rule 3.4. However, as discussed above, a prosecutor has special responsibilities in a criminal case. Model Rule 3.8.

D is incorrect. The prosecutor's responsibilities under Model Rule 3.8 exist independently of a request by defense counsel. The prosecutor's responsibility "carries with it specific obligations to see . . . that guilt is decided upon the basis of sufficient evidence." Model Rule 3.8, Comment [1].

Question 51.

A is the correct answer. A lawyer is prohibited from asking a person other than the client to refrain from voluntarily giving relevant information to another party unless that person is a relative, employee, or agent of the client and the lawyer reasonably believes that the person's interests will not be adversely affected by refraining to give that information.

Model Rule 3.4(f). In that case, the attorney may instruct the person to refrain from giving information unless subpoenaed. Here, the eyewitness did not fall under any of the exceptions to the rule.

B is incorrect. A lawyer is under no obligation to subpoena a witness that the lawyer does not intend to call at trial.

C is incorrect. Even if a witness has not yet been subpoenaed, Model Rule 3.4(f) prohibits an attorney from asking that witness to refrain from giving relevant information to another party, unless that witness falls within one of the three exceptions.

D is incorrect. Even though the attorney did not offer the witness any inducement not to appear at trial, the Rule prohibits the attorney from making any "request" to refrain from voluntarily giving relevant information.

Question 52.

A is the correct answer. A lawyer is prohibited from communicating about a matter with a person known to be represented in the matter unless the person's lawyer consents to the communication or the communication is authorized by law. Model Rule 4.2. The important point is that it is the *lawyer's* consent that is necessary, not the client's. In addition, a lawyer may not violate the rules directly or through the acts of another. Model Rule 8.4(a). Here, the attorney used a non-lawyer agent, the investigator, to violate the no-contact rule.

B is incorrect. The investigator merely relayed a communication from the attorney to the defendant and did not thereby engage in the unauthorized practice of law.

C is incorrect. As stated above, a lawyer is prohibited from communicating with a represented person whether the communication is performed by the attorney or an agent of the attorney. Here, the attorney cannot get around the rule by using a non-lawyer in making the communication.

D is incorrect. Here, the defendant's lawyer did not consent to the communication, and the fact the defendant's lawyer might not have relayed the settlement offer did not otherwise justify the communication.

Question 53.

B is the correct answer. A client who has given consent to a potential conflict of interest may revoke the consent and, like any other client, terminate the lawyer's representation at any time. Model Rule 1.7,

Comment [21]. Here, it was improper for the attorney to insist that the wife adhere to the prior agreement since she had an absolute right to terminate the joint representation.

A is incorrect. Under Model Rule 1.7, the initial representation was proper because it was reasonable for the attorney to believe that he was able to provide competent and diligent representation to both the husband and the wife, and both clients' consent was informed and in writing.

C is incorrect. Even though the clients initially consented to the joint representation, each had an absolute right at any time to revoke the consent and terminate the attorney's representation. Here, it was improper for the attorney to insist that the wife gave up that right. However, in some cases, a client's revocation of consent to a joint representation can effect whether the attorney can continue to represent the other client. Whether a client's revoked consent precludes the lawyer from continuing to represent other clients depends on the circumstances, "including the nature of the conflict, whether the client revoked consent because of a material change in circumstances, the reasonable expectations of the other client, and whether material detriment to the other clients or the lawyer would result." Model Rule 1.7, Comment [21].

D is incorrect. As stated above, whether the husband and wife independently made the agreement or not, they still had an absolute right to revoke their consent to the joint representation at any time.

Question 54.

D is the correct answer. A lawyer appearing before a legislative body must disclose that the appearance is in a representative capacity. Model Rule 3.9. This Rule recognizes the fact that a legislative body will likely give great weight to a lawyer's opinions on a question of law or legislative rule making. Requiring a lawyer to disclose the client relationship allows the legislative body to assess any potential bias of the lawyer.

A is incorrect. Here, the fact that the attorney believes her client's position is in the public interest does not cure the Rule violation. Always be wary of answer choices that imply a Rule was not violated because the attorney would have said or done the same thing despite the Rule violation.

B is incorrect. As stated above, the congressional members at the hearing would be very interested in knowing whether a witness is possibly biased in his or her testimony; therefore, Model Rule 3.9 requires a lawyer appearing in a representative capacity to disclose that fact to the legislative body.

C is incorrect. Lawyers frequently serve as paid lobbyists. This activity is permissible so long as the lawyer-lobbyist complies with applicable rules, such as the requirement to disclose his or her representative capacity when appearing before a legislative body.

Question 55.

D is the correct answer. A practicing lawyer who is also a legislator may not use his or her official authority for the benefit of a private client. However, a legislator who is a lawyer but who is no longer practicing law may assist a constituent in its dealings with a state agency. Here, the facts show that the senator is helping the bank as a constituent, not a client. Consequently, the senator's action would not subject her to discipline.

A is incorrect. Because the senator was assisting the bank as a constituent and not a client, she did not misuse her official position.

B is incorrect. The senator's efforts as a legislator on behalf of a constituent were proper because she was no longer practicing law and was not seeking to assist the bank as a private client. Therefore, it does not matter that the senator in fact influenced the agency in her former client's favor.

C is incorrect. The Rules do not prohibit a legislator who is also a lawyer from expressing opinions about the law.

Question 56.

C is the correct answer. Although a lawyer is not allowed to counsel or assist a client in criminal or fraudulent conduct, a lawyer may help a client determine the validity, scope, meaning, or application of the law to a client's particular situation. Model Rule 1.2(d). Here, the attorney is not helping the client break the law; she is simply delineating the law's boundaries.

A is incorrect. As long as a lawyer is not helping a client to violate the law, he or she is not required to make a guess as to how that client is going to use the lawyer's advice, nor is the attorney subject to discipline if the client decides to use the lawyer's advice to break the law. Here, the attorney simply gave her opinion regarding the parameters of the law.

B is incorrect. Here, the attorney specifically told the client that she would not tell him how to avoid detection. All she did was tell him about the law and its history. Although discouraging a client from violating the law might have been the best practice, failing to discourage him from violating the law is not cause for discipline.

D is incorrect. As stated above, lawyers may not assist clients in violating the law, and this includes discussing the best way to avoid detection.

Question 57.

D is the correct answer. Judges are permitted to consult with other judges on the court about pending cases as long as any consultation does not affect their responsibilities to personally decide the matters and as long as they make reasonable efforts to avoid receiving factual information that is not part of the record. Model Code of Judicial Conduct, Rule 2.9(A)(3).

A is incorrect. A conversation with another judge on the court about a pending matter does not count as an inappropriate ex parte communication.

B is incorrect. As stated above, a judge may consult with another judge in the court about a case, as long as the judge does not thereby give up his or her responsibility to personally decide the matter.

C is incorrect. Under the Model Code of Judicial Conduct, Rule 2.9(A)(2), a judge may obtain written advice from a disinterested expert provided that the judge gives advance notice to the parties about details of the consultation and the opportunity to object and respond to the advice. This rule, however, is not applicable to a situation in which a judge consults with another judge in the court.

Question 58.

B is the correct answer. This plan for part of the administrator's compensation to be based upon the net profits of the firm is expressly permitted under Model Rule 5.4(a) as long as the non-lawyer is an employee of the firm. Importantly, the other aspects of the arrangement do not give the administrator an inappropriate ownership interest in the firm, nor in any right to control the legal work done in the law firm, thus avoiding any violation of the Rule.

A is incorrect. The plan is proper, but the reason why it is proper has nothing to do with the compensation paid to other law office administrators in the community. This answer wrongly refers to Model Rule 1.5(a)'s guidelines on reasonable fees for lawyers, which list as one factor fees paid to other similarly situated lawyers in the community. Be wary of answer choices referring to standards in the local community, as these are often wrong.

C is incorrect. The Rules do not address the basis on which net profits may be divided and distributed to non-lawyer employees. Such decisions are properly made by the firm.

D is incorrect. Although lawyers may not share legal fees with non-lawyers, Model Rule 5.4(a) contains an exception for compensation plans that involve the sharing of net profits with non-lawyer employees.

Question 59.

D is the correct answer. The information regarding the perjury committed by the client's former partner is "information relating to the representation" of the client, which generally may not be disclosed without client consent. Model Rule 1.6(a). Confidential information may be disclosed without client consent under Model Rule 1.6(a) when "the disclosure is impliedly authorized in order to carry out the representation," but there would be no implied authorization where, as here, the disclosure would likely harm the client.

A is incorrect. The lawyer's duty to protect client information under Model Rule 1.6(a) covers more than just privileged information. It covers all "information relating to the representation of a client." Thus, it doesn't matter whether the information is privileged or not.

B is incorrect. Under Model Rule 3.3(b), if a lawyer is representing a client and offers material evidence (such as a person's testimony) that is later discovered to be false, that lawyer must take reasonable remedial measures, including, if necessary, disclosure to the tribunal. However, that duty does not apply here because the attorney did not represent the client in the proceeding where the client's former partner committed the perjury. Therefore, the attorney has no duty to disclose the perjury under Model Rule 3.3(b).

C is incorrect. The duties created by Model Rule 3.3(b) last only to the end of the case. Here, the case in which the former partner committed perjury is over. Consequently, even if the attorney had represented the client in that proceeding, the attorney would have no duty at this time to disclose the former partner's perjury. Importantly, if a lawyer first learns of the false evidence after the case is over, the duty of confidentiality under Model Rule 1.6 prohibits disclosure.

Question 60.

B is the correct answer. Because this is an aggregate settlement of all of the clients' claims, the attorney must obtain the clients' informed consent after disclosing "the existence and nature of all the claims" and "the participation of each person in the settlement." Model Rule 1.8(g). The necessary disclosure must include information about "all the material terms of the settlement, including what the other clients will receive or pay if the settlement or plea offer is accepted." Model Rule 1.8(g), Comment [13]. Even if the settlement could be jeopardized, Model Rule 1.2(a) protects each client's right to have the final say in deciding whether to accept or reject a settlement. Ultimately, it is not the lawyer's place to decide what is the best outcome for the clients.

A is incorrect. A lawyer may participate in an aggregate settlement of civil claims as long as the lawyer complies with the requirement of informed consent by all clients. Model Rule 1.8(g). Here, by not giving the clients all the information regarding what each one of them would receive under the settlement, the attorney failed to do so.

C is incorrect. As stated above, regardless of whether the settlement will be jeopardized, the clients need to know all the material terms of the settlement.

D is incorrect. The lawyer must still make a full disclosure to the clients whether or not the lawyer believes the aggregate settlement offer is fair, or whether or not the clients are satisfied with the amount. Always be wary of such "no harm, no foul" answer options.

Part Three
Sample NCBE Practice Questions

Part Two contained Model Answers to 60 of the Model Questions taken from the National Conference of Bar Examiner's **MPRE Sample Questions VI** and **MPRE — Online Practice Exam 1**. Below are 96 more practice questions taken from these two sources.

Answering the questions below will complete your preparation for the MPRE. Read each question carefully and circle the answer you think is correct. Then check your answer against the NCBE Answer Key on page 188.

If you selected the right answer, make sure you can articulate the reasons that led you to that answer (too often students check only their wrong answers, and fail to discover that they got a question right for the wrong reasons or simply made a lucky guess). Importantly, write down which of the Rules in the Model Rules or the Model Code of Judicial Conduct you relied on in reasoning your way to your answer.

If you selected one of the three wrong answers, you have some work to do. Ask yourself: Why am I wrong? What did I miss in the facts? How do I avoid making this mistake again? Importantly, figure out what Rule the question was testing you on, and write that down on your list. Highlight the ones you miss.

Once you've made this sheet of Rules, you should memorize it. The best way to do so (and educational studies going back to the 1960s support this) is to memorize the sheet, put it away, and then try to write it again from memory. Keep repeating this exercise until you can write out the entire sheet without a mistake.

Basically, if you review and re-review these questions and your own answers, there's a good chance you'll recognize essentially the same facts and issues in the questions on your own MPRE exam.

A. Practice Questions

1.

An attorney and a restaurant owner entered into a reciprocal referral arrangement. The attorney agreed to prominently display ads for the restaurant in her office, and to mention the restaurant to all of her clients who requested a recommendation of a nearby place to eat. In return, the owner agreed to prominently display ads for the attorney's firm in the restaurant and to recommend the attorney to any of his customers who indicated a need for the services provided by the attorney. The reciprocal referral agreement was not exclusive, and the clients and customers would be informed of the existence and nature of the agreement.

Is the attorney subject to discipline for entering into this agreement?

(A) Yes, because she asked the owner to place ads for the firm in the restaurant.

(B) Yes, because the agreement provided something of value to the restaurant owner in return for recommending the attorney's services.

(C) No, because she did not pay the restaurant owner for the referrals.

(D) No, because the agreement is not exclusive, and the clients and customers will be informed of the existence and nature of the agreement.

2.

Attorneys Alpha and Beta practiced law under the firm name of Alpha and Beta. When Beta died, Alpha did not change the firm name. Thereafter, Alpha entered into an arrangement with another attorney, Gamma. Gamma pays Alpha a certain sum each month for office space and use of Alpha's law library and for secretarial services, but Alpha and Gamma each has his own clients, and neither participates in the representation of the other's clients or shares in fees paid. On the entrance to the suite of offices shared by Alpha and Gamma are the words "Law Firm of Alpha, Beta, and Gamma."

Is Alpha subject to discipline?

(A) Yes, because Beta was deceased when Alpha made the arrangement with Gamma.

(B) Yes, because Gamma is not a partner of Alpha.

(C) No, because Alpha and Beta were partners at the time of Beta's death.

(D) No, because Gamma is paying a share of the rent and office expenses.

3.

An attorney was employed as a lawyer by the state Environmental Control Commission (ECC) for 10 years. During the last two years of her employment, the attorney spent most of her time in the preparation, trial, and appeal of a case involving the discharge by a corporation of industrial effluent into a river in the state. The judgment in the case, which is now final, contained a finding of a continuing and knowing discharge of a dangerous substance into a major stream by the corporation and assessed a penalty of $25,000.

The governing statute also provides for private actions for damages by persons injured by the discharge of the effluent.

The attorney recently left the employment of ECC and went into private practice. Three landowners have brought private damage actions against the corporation. They claim their farms were contaminated because they irrigated them with water that contained dangerous chemicals discharged by the corporation. The corporation has asked the attorney to represent it in defense of the three pending actions.

Is the attorney subject to discipline if she represents the corporation in these actions?

(A) Yes, unless the judgment in the prior case is determinative of the corporation's liability.

(B) Yes, because the attorney had substantial responsibility in the matter while employed by ECC.

(C) No, because the attorney has acquired special competence in the matter.

(D) No, if all information acquired by the attorney while representing ECC is now a matter of public record.

4.

An attorney is skilled in trying personal injury cases. The attorney accepted the representation of a plaintiff in a personal injury case on a contingent fee basis. While preparing the case for trial, the attorney realized that the direct examination and cross-examination of the medical experts would involve medical issues with which the attorney was not familiar and, as a consequence, the attorney might not be able to represent the plaintiff competently.

Without informing the plaintiff, the attorney consulted another attorney who is also a medical doctor and a recognized specialist in the care and treatment of injuries of the type sustained by the plaintiff. The two attorneys agreed that the other attorney would participate in the trial to the limited extent of conducting the direct examination and cross-examination of the medical experts and that the attorneys would divide the fee in proportion to the services performed and the responsibility assumed by each.

Was the arrangement between the two attorneys proper?

(A) Yes, because the fee to be paid by the plaintiff was not increased by reason of the other attorney's association.

(B) Yes, because the fee would be divided in proportion to the services performed and the responsibility assumed by each.

(C) No, because the plaintiff was not advised of the association of the other attorney.

(D) No, unless, upon conclusion of the matter, the attorney provides the plaintiff with a written statement setting forth the method of determining both the fee and the division of the fee with the other attorney.

5.

An attorney represents a famous politician in an action against a newspaper for libel. The case has attracted much publicity, and a jury trial has been demanded. After one of the pretrial hearings, as the attorney left the courthouse, news reporters interviewed the attorney. In responding to questions, the attorney revealed the identity of the reporter.

Is the attorney subject to discipline for making this statement?

(A) Yes, because the attorney identified a prospective witness in the case.

(B) Yes, because prospective jurors might learn of the attorney's remarks.

(C) No, because the statement relates to a matter of public record.

(D) No, because the trial has not commenced.

6.

An attorney was employed as an assistant prosecutor in the district attorney's office during the time that an investigation of a suspect was being conducted by that office. The attorney took no part in the investigation and had no knowledge of the facts other than those disclosed in the press. Two months ago, the attorney left the district attorney's office and formed a partnership with another attorney.

Last week, the suspect was indicted for offenses allegedly disclosed by the prior investigation. The suspect asked the attorney to represent him. The attorney declined to do so, but suggested his new partner.

Is the new partner subject to discipline if he represents the suspect?

(A) Yes, because the attorney was employed in the district attorney's office while the investigation of the suspect was being conducted.

(B) Yes, unless the district attorney's office is promptly notified and consents to the representation.

(C) No, unless the attorney participates in the representation or shares in the fee.

(D) No, because the attorney had no responsibility for or knowledge of the facts of the investigation of the suspect.

7.

A defendant was on trial for murder. The victim was killed during a barroom brawl. In the course of closing arguments to the jury, the prosecutor said,

"The defendant's whole defense is based on the testimony of his friend, who said that the victim attacked the defendant with a knife before the defendant struck him. No other witness testified to such an attack by the victim. I don't believe the defendant's friend was telling the truth, and I don't think you believe him either."

Was the prosecutor's statement proper?

(A) Yes, if the prosecutor accurately stated the testimony in the case.

(B) Yes, if the prosecutor, in fact, believed the defendant's friend was lying.

(C) No, because the prosecutor alluded to the beliefs of the jurors.

(D) No, because the prosecutor asserted his personal opinion about the defendant's credibility.

8.

An attorney represents a plaintiff in a civil action that was filed a year ago and is about to be set for trial. The plaintiff informed the attorney that he could be available at any time during the months of October, November, and December. In discussing possible trial dates with opposing counsel and the court clerk, the attorney was advised that a trial date on October 5 was available and that the next available trial date would be December 10. Without first consulting the plaintiff, the attorney requested the December 10 trial date because she was representing a defendant in a felony criminal trial that was set for October 20 and she wanted as much time as possible to prepare for that trial.

Was it proper for the attorney to agree to the December trial date without obtaining the plaintiff's consent?

(A) Yes, unless the plaintiff will be prejudiced by the delay.

(B) Yes, because a criminal trial takes precedence over a civil trial.

(C) No, because the attorney should manage her calendar so that her cases can be tried promptly.

(D) No, unless the attorney was court-appointed counsel in the criminal case.

9.

Three men were indicted for the armed robbery of the cashier of a grocery store. Together, two of them met with an attorney and asked the attorney to represent them. The attorney then interviewed the two of them separately. Each told the attorney that the robbery had been committed by the third man while they sat in the third man's car outside the store. They also said that the third man had said he needed some cigarettes, and that neither knew of the man's plan to rob the cashier. The attorney agreed to the joint representation. One week prior to the trial date, one of the men represented by the attorney told the attorney that he wanted to plea bargain and that he was prepared to turn state's evidence against both of the other two suspects.

It is proper for attorney to:

(A) request court approval to withdraw as lawyer for both men.

(B) continue to represent the man who had not stated that he wanted to plea bargain and, with the other man's consent and court approval, withdraw as his lawyer.

(C) continue to represent the man who wanted to plea bargain and, with the other man's consent and court approval, withdraw as that man's lawyer.

(D) continue to represent both men, but not call the man who wanted to plea bargain as a witness.

10.

While presiding over the trial of a highly publicized antitrust case, a judge received in the mail a lengthy letter from a local attorney. The letter discussed the law applicable to the case. The judge knew that the attorney did not represent either party. The judge read the letter and, without mentioning its receipt to the lawyers in the pending case, filed the letter in his general file on antitrust litigation.

Later, after reading the trial briefs in the case, the judge concluded that the attorney's letter better explained the law applicable to the case pending before him than either of the trial briefs. The judge followed the attorney's reasoning in formulating his decision.

Was it proper for the judge to consider the attorney's letter?

(A) Yes, because the judge did not initiate the communication with the attorney.

(B) Yes, if the attorney did not represent any client whose interests could be affected by the outcome.

(C) No, unless the judge, prior to rendering his decision, communicated its contents to all counsel and gave them an opportunity to respond.

(D) No, because the attorney is not of record as counsel in the case.

11.

An attorney's recorded radio advertisement stated:

"For a fee of $600 I will represent a party to a divorce that does not result in a court trial of a contested issue of fact."

The attorney had the advertisement prerecorded and approved by the appropriate bar agency for broadcast. The attorney retained a recording of the actual transmission in her office. A woman who had previously agreed with her husband to an uncontested dissolution of their marriage heard the broadcast and called on the attorney in the attorney's office. She told the attorney that she had heard the broadcast and asked the attorney to represent her. The attorney agreed to the representation. Because of the nature of the parties' property, the attorney spent more time on the tax aspects of the case than the attorney anticipated. The time expended by the attorney, if charged at a reasonable hourly rate, would have resulted in a fee of $2,000. After the decree was entered, the attorney billed his client for $2,000.

Is the attorney subject to discipline?

(A) No, because the attorney's fee was a reasonable charge for the time expended.

(B) No, because the attorney, when the representation was accepted, did not anticipate the tax problems.

(C) Yes, unless the client pays the fee without protest.

(D) Yes, because the attorney charged a fee in excess of the advertised fee.

12.

A certified public accountant proposed to an attorney who is a recognized specialist in the field of tax law, that the accountant and the attorney form a partnership for the purpose of providing clients with tax-related legal and accounting services. Both the accountant and the attorney have deserved reputations of being competent, honest, and trustworthy. The accountant further proposes that the announcement of the proposed partnership, the firm stationery, and all public directory listings clearly state that the accountant is a certified public accountant and that the attorney is a lawyer.

Is the attorney subject to discipline if he enters into the proposed partnership with the accountant?

(A) Yes, because one of the activities of the partnership would be providing legal services to clients.

(B) Yes, because the attorney would be receiving fees paid for other than legal services.

(C) No, because the partnership will assure to the public high-quality services in the fields of tax law and accounting.

(D) No, if the attorney is the only person in the partnership who gives advice on legal matters.

13.

A client retained an attorney to appeal his criminal conviction and to seek bail pending appeal. The agreed-upon fee for the appearance on the bail hearing was $100 per hour. The attorney received $1,600 from the client, of which $600 was a deposit to secure the attorney's fee and $1,000 was for bail costs in the event that bail was obtained. The attorney maintained two office bank accounts: a fee account, in which all fees collected from clients were deposited and from which all office expenses were paid, and a clients' trust account. The attorney deposited the $1,600 in the clients' trust account the week before the bail hearing. She expended six hours of her time preparing for and appearing at the hearing. The effort to obtain bail was unsuccessful. Dissatisfied, the client immediately demanded return of the $1,600.

What should the attorney do with the $1,600?

(A) Transfer the $1,600 to the fee account.

(B) Transfer the $600 to the fee account and leave $1,000 in the clients' trust account until the attorney's fee for the final appeal is determined.

(C) Transfer $600 to the fee account and send the client a $1,000 check on the clients' trust account.

(D) Send the client a $1,000 check and leave $600 in the clients' trust account until the matter is resolved with the client.

14.

An attorney represents a client in commercial litigation that is scheduled to go to trial in two months. Over the past several weeks, the client has disagreed with almost every tactical decision that the attorney has made. Frustrated, the attorney finally said to the client that if she didn't like the way he was handling the lawsuit, perhaps she should get another lawyer. The client was upset at the suggestion and accused the attorney of trying to get out of the case. Reasonably believing that he could no longer work effectively with the client, the attorney sought the client's permission to withdraw from the representation, and the client reluctantly agreed. After giving the client sufficient notice to obtain replacement counsel, the attorney requested the court's permission to withdraw from the litigation, but the court denied the request.

May the attorney withdraw from the representation?

(A) Yes, because the client agreed, and the attorney gave the client sufficient notice to obtain replacement counsel.

(B) Yes, because the client had made it unreasonably difficult for the attorney to carry out the representation effectively.

(C) No, because the court denied the attorney's request to withdraw.

(D) No, because the attorney's withdrawal would cause material prejudice to the client, and the client's agreement was not voluntary.

15.

An attorney is employed in the legal department of a public utility company and represents that company in litigation. The company has been sued by a consumer group that has accused the company of various acts in violation of its charter. Through its general counsel, the company has instructed the attorney not to negotiate a settlement but to go to trial under any circumstances because a precedent needs to be established. The attorney believes the defense can be supported by a good faith argument, but also believes the case should be settled if possible.

Must the attorney withdraw as counsel in this case?

(A) Yes, because the company is controlling the attorney's judgment in refusing to settle the case.

(B) Yes, because a lawyer should endeavor to avoid litigation.

(C) No, because the company's defense can be supported by a good faith argument.

(D) No, because as an employee, the attorney is bound by the instruction of the general counsel.

16.

An attorney represented a plaintiff in an action for defamation against a defendant. After the defendant's lawyer had filed and served an answer, the attorney, at the plaintiff's direction, hired a licensed private investigator and instructed him to attempt to interview the defendant without revealing his employment. The investigator succeeded in interviewing the defendant privately and obtained an admission from the defendant that the statements the defendant had made were based solely on unsubstantiated gossip.

Is the attorney subject to discipline for obtaining the statement from the defendant in this matter?

(A) No, because the attorney was following the plaintiff's instructions.

(B) No, because the statement obtained was evidence that the defendant's allegations were unfounded.

(C) Yes, because the attorney should have interviewed the defendant personally.

(D) Yes, because the attorney instructed the investigator to interview the defendant.

17.

An attorney was retained by a woman to advise her in negotiating a separation agreement with her husband. The husband, who was not a lawyer, had decided to act on his own behalf in the matter. The attorney never met or communicated with the husband during the negotiations. After several months, the woman advised the attorney that the parties had reached agreement and presented him with the terms. The attorney prepared a proposed agreement that contained all of the agreed-upon terms. The attorney mailed the proposed agreement to the husband, with a cover letter stating:

> "As you know, I represent your wife in this matter and I do not represent your interests. I enclose two copies of the separation agreement that I have drafted in accordance with my client's directions. Please read the agreement and, if it meets with your approval, sign both copies before a notary and return them to me. I will then have your wife sign them and will furnish you with a fully executed copy."

Is the attorney subject to discipline?

(A) Yes, because the attorney did not suggest that the husband seek the advice of independent counsel before signing the agreement.

(B) Yes, because the attorney directly communicated with an unrepresented person.

(C) No, because the attorney acted only as a scrivener.

(D) No, because the attorney's letter did not imply that the attorney was disinterested and the attorney did not give legal advice to the husband.

18.

A judge, prior to her appointment to the probate court, was a partner in a law firm. The law firm had an extensive probate practice. At the time of the judge's appointment, the law firm had pending before the court to which the judge was appointed numerous matters in which requests were being made for allowances for attorney's fees. When the judge left the law firm, she was paid a cash settlement. She has no further financial interest in any matter handled by the law firm. The judge is now being asked to rule on these requests for allowances for attorney's fees.

Is it proper for the judge to rule on these requests?

(A) Yes, because the judge has no financial interest in the outcome of these cases.

(B) Yes, if these requests are not contested.

(C) No, unless the judge notes on the record in each case her prior association with the law firm.

(D) No, because the judge was associated with the law firm when these matters were pending.

19.

An attorney's law firm regularly represented a large company in its international business transactions. The company became involved in a contractual dispute with a foreign government. The company invoked a mandatory arbitration procedure contained in the contract. Under the arbitration clause, each party was allowed to choose a partisan arbitrator and the partisan arbitrators were to choose an additional arbitrator to sit on the panel. The company selected the attorney to be on the arbitration panel. Neither the attorney nor his law firm had represented the company in connection with the contract with the foreign government. The arbitration was completed, and the company was awarded the sum of $100,000. The company then hired the attorney to enforce the award. The attorney obtained the consent of the other arbitrators before accepting the representation. He was successful in enforcing the award.

Is the attorney subject to discipline?

(A) Yes, because the attorney should not have represented the company in a matter in which the attorney had been an arbitrator.

(B) Yes, because the attorney should have declined the arbitration assignment in view of his law firm's regular representation of the company.

(C) No, because the attorney obtained the consent of the other arbitrators before accepting the representation.

(D) No, because the attorney was appointed to the arbitration panel as a partisan arbitrator.

20.

An attorney represented a client who was injured when the television antenna he was attempting to erect in his yard came in contact with a power line. As part of its defense, the manufacturer of the antenna claimed that the antenna came with a warning label advising against erecting the antenna near power lines. The client told the attorney that he had not seen a warning label. The client's wife told the attorney that she had kept the antenna and the box it came in and that she saw no warning label anywhere.

When called by the attorney as witnesses, both the client and his wife testified that they had never seen a warning label. After their testimony, but while the trial was still in progress, the attorney learned from the wife's sister that there indeed had been a warning label on the box, but that the wife had removed and destroyed it. When the attorney confronted the wife with her sister's statement, the wife admitted destroying the label but insisted that her husband knew nothing about it. The attorney continued the trial, but made no reference to the absence of a warning label in his summation to the jury. Instead, the attorney argued that the warning label, even if seen, was insufficient to advise his client of the serious consequences that would ensue if the warning was not heeded. The jury found in favor of the manufacturer.

Is the attorney subject to discipline?

(A) Yes, because the attorney called the wife as a witness and she gave perjured testimony.

(B) Yes, because the attorney failed to take reasonable remedial action after he realized that the wife had given perjured testimony.

(C) No, because the jury apparently disbelieved the wife's testimony.

(D) No, because the attorney did not rely on the wife's testimony once he discovered the perjury.

21.

The attorney represented a client in a claim involving a breach of the client's employment contract. The case was settled without suit being filed. The proceeds of the settlement were paid directly to the client, who subsequently paid the attorney in full for the attorney's fee and expenses. Thereafter, the attorney did no other work for the client.

The client is now being audited by the Internal Revenue Service (IRS). The IRS has asked the attorney for details of the settlement, including the amount claimed for each item of damage and the amounts paid for the items. The attorney reported the request to the client, who told the attorney not to provide the information to the IRS.

Is it proper for the attorney to furnish the information to the IRS?

(A) Yes, if the information does not involve the attorney's work product.

(B) Yes, because the attorney no longer represents the client.

(C) No, because the client told the attorney not to provide the information.

(D) No, unless the attorney believes the disclosure would be beneficial to the client.

22.

An attorney and a licensed real estate broker entered into an agreement whereby the broker was to recommend the attorney to any customer of the broker who needed legal services, and the attorney was to recommend the broker to any client of the attorney who wished to buy or sell real estate. The attorney's practice is limited almost entirely to real estate law.

Is the attorney subject to discipline for entering into the agreement with the broker?

(A) Yes, because the attorney is compensating the broker for recommending the attorney's legal services.

(B) Yes, because the arrangement constitutes the practice of law in association with a non-lawyer.

(C) No, if neither the attorney nor the broker shares in the other's fees.

(D) No, if the fees of the attorney and the broker do not clearly exceed reasonable fees for the services rendered by each.

23.

An attorney represented a respondent in proceedings instituted by a child protection services agency to establish the paternity of a child and to recover past-due child support. The mother of the child had refused to file a complaint, had refused to retain a lawyer, and in fact had asked that the agency not file any action whatsoever. However, state law permitted the agency to commence paternity and support proceedings in its own name in such circumstances.

The attorney contacted the mother without the knowledge or consent of the agency or its lawyers. The attorney identified himself to the mother as "an officer of the court" and told the mother that he was investigating the matter. Based upon what she told him, the attorney prepared and the mother signed an affidavit truthfully stating that the respondent was not the father of the child.

Is the attorney subject to discipline?

(A) Yes, because the attorney acted without the knowledge or consent of the agency or its lawyers.

(B) Yes, because the attorney implied that he was disinterested in the matter.

(C) No, because all of the attorney's statements to the mother were true.

(D) No, because the attorney did not give the mother legal advice.

24.

An attorney in his capacity as part-time assistant county attorney represented the county in a criminal non-support proceeding against a defendant. This proceeding concluded with an order directing the defendant to pay or be jailed. The defendant refused to pay.

The attorney, pursuant to applicable rules, is permitted to maintain a private law practice. The defendant's ex-wife has discovered some assets of the defendant. The attorney now has accepted employment from the defendant's ex-wife to maintain a civil action against the defendant to recover out of those assets arrearages due to the ex-wife under the ex-wife's support decree. The attorney did not obtain consent from the county attorney or from the defendant to represent the ex-wife in the civil action.

Is the attorney subject to discipline for accepting employment in the ex-wife's civil action against the defendant?

(A) Yes, because the attorney did not obtain the defendant's consent to the representation.

(B) Yes, because the attorney had personal and substantial responsibility in the first proceeding.

(C) No, because the attorney's responsibility in his public employment has terminated.

(D) No, because the attorney is representing the ex-wife's interest in both the criminal and the civil proceedings.

25.

An attorney is a lawyer for the city and advises the city on all tort claims filed against it. The attorney's advice is limited to recommending settlement and the amount thereof. If a claim is not settled and suit is filed, defense of the suit is handled either by lawyers for the city's insurance carrier or by outside counsel specially retained for that purpose. In connection with any notice of claim and before suit is filed, the attorney arranges for an investigator to call upon the claimant at the claimant's home and, with no one else present, to interview the claimant and endeavor to obtain a signed statement of the claimant's version of the facts.

A claimant has filed a notice of claim against the city. The attorney has sent an investigator to interview the claimant.

Is the attorney subject to discipline for arranging an interview with the claimant?

(A) Yes, if the claimant was known by the attorney to be represented by counsel.

(B) Yes, if the statement taken is later used to the claimant's disadvantage.

(C) No, because the claimant had not filed suit at the time of the interview.

(D) No, because the attorney would not be representing the city in any subsequent litigation on the claimant's claim.

26.

An attorney joined a professional corporation engaged solely in the practice of law. As a salaried associate, she is not a member or shareholder of the professional corporation. One of the partner's spouses, who is not a lawyer, is vice-president of the corporation and office manager. All of the other officers are lawyers in the firm. All of the corporate shares are held by lawyers in the corporation, except for 10 shares held by the executor under the will of a lawyer-member who died one month previously and whose will is now being probated. The attorney knows that the partner's wife is an officer and not a lawyer.

Is the attorney subject to discipline?

(A) Yes, because the partner's wife is an officer of the corporation.

(B) Yes, if a non-lawyer holds the stock as the executor of the will of the deceased member.

(C) No, because the attorney is a salaried employee and not a member or shareholder of the corporation.

(D) No, if the partner's wife does not participate in any decision regarding a client or a client's case.

27.

An attorney is representing a plaintiff in a paternity suit against a defendant. Both the plaintiff and the defendant are well-known public figures, and the suit has attracted much publicity. The attorney has been billing the plaintiff at an agreed hourly fee for his services. Recently, the plaintiff told the attorney,

> "I'm going broke paying you. Why don't you let me assign you all media rights to books, movies, or television programs based on my suit as full payment for all services you will render me between now and the conclusion of the suit?"

The attorney replied,

> "I'll consider it, but first you should seek independent advice about whether such an arrangement is in your own best interests. Why don't you do so and call me next week."

Is the attorney subject to discipline if he agrees to the plaintiff's offer?

(A) Yes, because the amount received by the attorney would be contingent on the receipts from the sale of media rights.

(B) Yes, because the attorney has not concluded the representation of the plaintiff.

(C) No, because the paternity suit is a civil and not a criminal matter.

(D) No, if the plaintiff received independent advice before entering into the agreement.

28.

Four years ago, an attorney represented a husband and wife, both high school teachers, in the purchase of a new home. Since then, the attorney prepared their tax returns and drafted their wills.

Recently, the husband called the attorney and told her that he and his wife had decided to divorce, but wanted the matter to be resolved amicably. The husband stated that they were planning to file and process their own divorce case, utilizing the state's new streamlined divorce procedure, applicable in "no-fault" cases where there are no minor children. The husband asked if the attorney would agree to work with them to prepare a financial settlement agreement that could be presented to the divorce court, reminding the attorney that the couple's assets were modest and that they wanted to "split it all down the middle."

After considering the risks of a conflict of interest arising in this limited representation, the attorney wrote to the couple separately, and advised each that he or she might be better off with separate lawyers, but that the attorney would assist with the financial settlement agreement, charging an hourly fee of $140 per hour, provided that they were in complete agreement and remained so. The attorney advised that if a conflict developed, or if either party was dissatisfied or uncomfortable about continuing with the joint representation, the attorney would withdraw and would not represent either party from that point forward, forcing them to start all over again with separate lawyers. Finally, the attorney cautioned the husband and wife that the attorney would be representing both of them equally, would not and could not favor one or the other, and that their separate communications to her could not be kept confidential from the other party. Both the husband and the wife signed their individual copy of the letter, consenting to the joint representation, and returned them to the attorney.

Was it proper for the attorney to accept the representation on these terms?

(A) Yes, because there was little risk that the interests of either the husband or the wife would be materially prejudiced if no settlement was reached.

(B) Yes, because the attorney had previously represented the husband and the wife in their joint affairs.

(C) No, because the attorney conditioned representation upon receiving a waiver of client confidentially.

(D) No, unless the attorney advised both the husband and the wife, in writing, that they should seek independent counsel before agreeing to enter into the financial settlement on the terms proposed.

29.

An attorney represented a client in negotiating a large real estate trans-action. The buyer who purchased the real estate from the client has filed suit against both the client and the attorney, alleging fraud and violation of the state unfair trade practices statute. The attorney had advised the client by letter against making the statements that are the basis for the buyer's claim. The attorney and the client are each represented by separate counsel. In responding to a deposition under subpoena, the attorney wishes to reveal, to the extent the attorney reasonably believes necessary to defend herself, confidential information imparted to the attorney by the client that will be favorable to the attorney but damaging to the client.

Is it proper for the attorney to reveal such information?

(A) Yes, unless the client objects to the disclosure.

(B) Yes, because the attorney may reveal such information to defend herself against a civil claim.

(C) No, unless criminal charges have also been brought against the attorney.

(D) No, because the disclosure will be detrimental to the client.

30.

An attorney, who is corporate counsel for a company, is investigating a possible theft ring in the parts department of the company. The attorney knows that an employee has worked in the parts department a long time and believes that the employee is a suspect in the thefts. The attorney believes that if the employee were questioned, the employee would not answer truthfully if she knew the real purpose of the questions. The attorney plans to question the employee and falsely tell her that she is not a suspect and that her answers to the questions will be held in confidence.

Is the attorney subject to discipline if she so questions the employee?

(A) Yes, because the attorney's conduct involves misrepresentation.

(B) Yes, unless the attorney first advises the employee to obtain counsel.

(C) No, because no legal proceedings are now pending.

(D) No, because the attorney did not give legal advice to the employee.

31.

A manufacturer sued a parts company for breach of warranty regarding machine components furnished by the parts company. A judge, who presided at the non-jury trial, sent her law clerk to the manufacturer's plant to observe the machine that was malfunctioning due to the allegedly defective parts. The clerk returned and told the judge that the machine was indeed malfunctioning and that one of the manufacturer's engineers had explained to the clerk how the parts delivered by the parts company caused the malfunction. There was testimony at the trial that supported what the clerk learned on his visit. The judge rendered a judgment for the manufacturer.

Was the judge's conduct proper?

(A) Yes, because the judge's judgment was supported by evidence at the trial.

(B) Yes, because the judge has the right to gather facts concerning the trial.

(C) No, because the judge has engaged in ex parte contacts that might influence the outcome of litigation.

(D) No, unless the engineer was a witness at the trial and subject to cross-examination by the parts company.

32.

When one of an attorney's regular clients planned to leave on a world tour, the client delivered to the attorney sufficient money to pay the client's property taxes when they became due. The attorney placed the money in her Clients' Trust Account. When the tax payment date arrived, the attorney was in need of a temporary loan to close the purchase of a new personal residence. Because the penalty for late payment of taxes was only 2 percent while the rate for a personal loan was 6 percent, the attorney withdrew the client's funds from the trust account to cover the attorney's personal check for the closing. The attorney was confident that the client would not object. Ten days later, after the receipt of a large fee previously earned, the attorney paid the client's property taxes and the 2 percent penalty, fully satisfying the client's tax obligation. After the client returned, the attorney told the client what she had done, and the client approved the attorney's conduct.

Is the attorney subject to discipline?

(A) Yes, because the attorney failed to pay the client the 10 days of interest at the fair market rate.

(B) Yes, because the attorney used the client's funds for a personal purpose.

(C) No, because the client was not harmed and the attorney reasonably believed at the time she withdrew the money that the client would not object.

(D) No, because when the attorney told the client what she had done, the client approved the attorney's conduct.

33.

An attorney entered into a written retainer agreement with a defendant in a criminal case. The defendant agreed in writing to transfer title to the defendant's automobile to the attorney if the attorney successfully prevented him from going to prison. Later, the charges against the defendant were dismissed.

Is the attorney subject to discipline for entering into this retainer agreement?

(A) Yes, because the attorney agreed to a fee contingent on the outcome of a criminal case.

(B) Yes, because a lawyer may not acquire a proprietary interest in a client's property.

(C) No, because the charges against the defendant were dismissed.

(D) No, because the retainer agreement is in writing.

34.

An attorney filed a complaint on behalf of her client against a corporation, alleging that the corporation had breached a valid oral contract entered into on the corporation's behalf by its president and chief executive officer. The attorney representing the corporation has filed an answer denying the contract and asserting the statute of frauds as a defense.

The corporation's attorney has given notice that he will take the deposition of the corporation's president on the grounds that he will be out of the country on the date the case is set for trial. The corporation's president is not a shareholder of the corporation. The attorney would like to interview the corporation's president prior to the taking of the deposition in order better to prepare her cross-examination.

Is the attorney subject to discipline if she interviews the corporation's president without the corporation's attorney's knowledge and consent?

(A) No, unless the corporation president will be personally liable to the corporation for damages in the event judgment is rendered against the corporation.

(B) No, because the corporation's president allegedly entered into the contract on behalf of the corporation.

(C) Yes, because the corporation's president is being called as an adverse witness.

(D) Yes, because the corporation's president is president of the corporation.

35.

An attorney agreed to represent a client in a lawsuit. The attorney and the client executed the attorney's preprinted retainer form that provides, in part:

> "The client agrees to pay promptly the attorney's fee for services. In addition, the client and the attorney agree to release each other from any and all liability arising from the representation. The client agrees that the attorney need not return the client's file prior to receiving the client's executed release. Upon full payment, the attorney will return the file to the client."

Although the attorney recommended that the client consult independent counsel before signing the retainer agreement, the client chose not to do so. The attorney reasonably believes that his fee is fair and that the quality of his work will be competent.

Is the attorney's retainer agreement with the client proper?

(A) Yes, because the attorney furnished consideration by agreeing to return the client's file.

(B) Yes, because the attorney reasonably believes that his fee is fair and that the quality of his work will be competent.

(C) No, because the attorney is attempting to limit his liability for malpractice.

(D) No, because the attorney uses a preprinted form for all retainers.

36.

An attorney serves on a bar association committee established to counsel and rehabilitate lawyers who suffer from substance abuse. The day before the attorney was to leave on a fishing trip, the attorney's close friend, another attorney, disclosed to the attorney that, over the preceding two years, he had become heavily addicted to cocaine and was afraid he had committed criminal offenses in his banking activities as a result of his addiction. He then asked the attorney to represent him. The attorney agreed, but explained that he could do little for two weeks and would consult with his friend immediately upon his return. While on the fishing trip, an accountant who knew that the attorney was going to represent his friend told him that the accountant had been retained by the trust department of a commercial bank to audit several substantial trust accounts in which the bank and the attorney's friend are co-trustees. The accountant also told the attorney that the audit furnished incontrovertible proof that the attorney's friend had embezzled more than $100,000 from the trust accounts.

Must the attorney report his friend's embezzlement to the appropriate disciplinary authority?

(A) Yes, because the attorney learned of his friend's embezzlement from the accountant.

(B) Yes, because the attorney's failure to report would assist the concealment of his friend's breach of trust.

(C) No, because the attorney gained the information while representing his friend.

(D) No, because the information will probably be made public by the bank.

37.

The following advertisement appeared in a daily newspaper in a state in which both parties are members of the bar:

A. ALPHA, M.D., J.D.

and

B. BETA, J.D.

Attorneys at Law

1000 "A" Street, City, State, 00000

Telephone (555) 555-5555

Are Alpha and Beta subject to discipline?

(A) No, because both law and medicine are licensed professions.

(B) No, if they possess the degree(s) stated.

(C) Yes, because the reference to the M.D. degree is self-laudatory.

(D) Yes, unless they limit their practice to areas in which a medical degree is relevant.

38.

While working on a complex matter for her client, an attorney, a partner in a law firm, identified a particularly difficult issue of law that could prove decisive in the dispute. The attorney had not encountered this issue before and was uncertain of its effect. The attorney asked her partner for assistance.

Was it proper for the attorney to consult with her partner?

(A) No, unless the total fee is not increased by the consultation.

(B) No, because the client's consent was not previously obtained.

(C) Yes, unless the attorney identified the client to her partner.

(D) Yes, because the attorney and her partner are partners in the same firm.

39.

A state court judge has presided over the pretrial proceedings in a case involving a novel contract question under the Uniform Commercial

Code. During the pretrial proceedings, the judge has acquired considerable background knowledge of the facts and law of the matter and, therefore, is particularly well qualified to preside at the trial. Shortly before the trial date, the judge discovered that his brother owns a substantial block of stock in the defendant corporation. He determined that his brother's financial interests would be substantially affected by the outcome of the case. Although the judge believed he would be impartial, he disclosed to the parties, on the record, his brother's interest.

Is it proper for the judge to hear the case?

(A) Yes, because the judge is particularly well qualified to preside at the trial.

(B) Yes, because the judge believes his judgment will not be affected by his brother's stockholding.

(C) No, because disqualification based on a relative's financial interest cannot be waived.

(D) No, unless after proper proceedings in which the judge did not participate all parties and their lawyers consent in writing that the judge may hear the case.

40.

An attorney is representing a client on a charge of armed robbery. The client claims that the prosecution witness is mistaken in her identification. The client has produced a witness who will testify that the client was in another city 500 miles away when the robbery occurred. The attorney knows that the witness is lying, but the client insists that the witness be called on the client's behalf.

Is the attorney subject to discipline if she calls the witness?

(A) Yes, unless, before calling the witness, the attorney informs the court of her belief.

(B) Yes, because the attorney knows the witness will be testifying falsely.

(C) No, unless the attorney relies on the alibi defense in her argument before the jury.

(D) No, because the client has insisted that the witness be called as a witness on the client's behalf.

41.

A recently graduated attorney began a plaintiffs' personal injury practice, but was having a difficult time attracting clients. The attorney hired an advertising agency to prepare a television commercial in which the attorney appeared to be arguing a case before a jury. In the commercial, the jury brought back a large award for the attorney's client. The voice-over stated that results would vary depending upon particular legal and factual circumstances. The attorney's only experience at the time the commercial was filmed was in moot court. As a result of airing the commercial, the attorney received several significant cases.

Is the attorney subject to discipline?

(A) Yes, because the commercial created an unjustified expectation about the results that could be achieved in court.

(B) Yes, because the commercial implied that the attorney had successfully argued a case to a jury.

(C) No, because commercial speech is protected under the First Amendment.

(D) No, because the commercial contained an express disclaimer about the results a client could expect.

42.

The state bar association has offered a judge and her spouse free transportation and lodging to attend its institute on judicial reform. The judge is expected to deliver a banquet speech.

Is it proper for the judge to accept this offer?

(A) Yes, unless the value of the transportation and lodging exceeds $500.

(B) Yes, because the activity is devoted to the improvement of law.

(C) No, if members of the bar association regularly appear in the judge's court.

(D) No, because the bar association is offering free transportation to the judge's spouse.

43.

An attorney regularly appears before a trial court judge who is running for reelection in six months. Over the past year, the attorney has noticed that the judge has become increasingly ill-tempered on the bench. Not only is the judge abrupt and critical of lawyers appearing before him, he is also rude and abusive to litigants. On more than one occasion, the judge has thrown his gavel across the courtroom in a fit of temper. The judge's conduct on the bench is often the subject of discussion whenever a group of lawyers meets. Some lawyers are automatically filing requests for judicial substitution whenever a case in which they are to appear is assigned to the judge.

The attorney discussed the matter with her law partners, who rarely make court appearances. The attorney's law partners suggested that she also file a request for judicial substitution whenever one of her cases is assigned to the judge. In addition, the attorney and her law partners discussed the possibility of reporting the judge to the appropriate disciplinary authority but are concerned that this would alienate the other judges to whom their cases are assigned. The attorney has reluctantly started filing for substitution of the judge in every one of her cases to which the judge is assigned, but she has taken no further action.

Is the attorney subject to discipline?

(A) Yes, because the attorney failed to inform the appropriate authorities about the judge's conduct.

(B) Yes, because, by filing automatic requests for substitution of the judge, the attorney undermined public confidence in the administration of justice.

(C) No, because the attorney has a duty to represent her clients zealously.

(D) No, because the judge is running for reelection and may not be reelected.

44.

Leaving an airport, an attorney who primarily practices criminal law shared a cab with a medical doctor. The cab was involved in a collision, and the doctor was seriously injured, while the attorney was only shaken up. The attorney accompanied the doctor to the hospital in the ambulance. The doctor believed that she was dying and asked the attorney to prepare a simple will for her. The attorney told the doctor, "I have never prepared a will, but hope that I can remember the basics from law school." The attorney then complied with the doctor's request. The doctor signed the will, and the two paramedics in the ambulance signed as witnesses.

Was it proper for the attorney to prepare the will?

(A) Yes, unless the attorney omitted some required formality that rendered the will invalid.

(B) Yes, because the attorney provided legal services that were reasonably necessary under the circumstances.

(C) No, unless the doctor waived the attorney's malpractice liability.

(D) No, because the attorney did not have the skill required for the representation.

45.

An attorney has recently started her own law firm with four other lawyers as associates. The law firm has moved into offices in a new building which is owned by a bank. The attorney has borrowed heavily from the bank to finance her new law firm. In addition, the bank provides the law firm with accounting services through its computer.

At the bank's suggestion, an employee of the bank, who is not a lawyer, serves as a part-time office manager for the law firm without compensation from the firm. The duties of the office manager are to advise the firm generally on fees and time charges, program matters for the computer services, and consult with the attorney on accounting and billing practices to ensure solvency.

Is the arrangement with the bank proper?

(A) Yes, unless secrets or confidences of clients may be disclosed to the bank.

(B) Yes, because the office manager is paid by the bank.

(C) No, because a non-lawyer will be advising the law firm on fees and time charges.

(D) No, because the bank will be involved in the practice of law.

46.

An attorney is representing the plaintiff in a personal injury case, on a contingent fee basis. The client is without resources to pay for the expenses of the investigation and the medical examinations necessary to prepare for trial. The client asked the attorney to pay for these expenses. The attorney declined to advance the funds but offered to guarantee the client's promissory note to a local bank in order to secure the funds needed to cover those expenses. The client has agreed to reimburse the attorney in the event the attorney incurs liability on the guaranty.

Is the attorney subject to discipline if she guarantees the client's promissory note?

(A) Yes, because the attorney is lending her credit to the client.

(B) Yes, because the attorney is helping to finance litigation.

(C) No, because the funds will be used for trial preparation.

(D) No, because the attorney took the case on a contingent fee basis.

47.

An attorney represents a defendant in an action for personal injuries. The attorney, pursuant to the defendant's authorization, made an offer of settlement to the attorney who represents the plaintiff. The plaintiff's attorney has not responded to the offer, and the attorney is convinced that the plaintiff's attorney has not communicated the offer to the plaintiff. State law authorizes a defendant to move for a settlement conference and to tender an offer of settlement. If such a motion is made and the offer is rejected by the plaintiff and the eventual judgment does not exceed the amount of the offer, the plaintiff must bear all costs of litigation, including reasonable fees, as determined by the court, for the defendant's counsel.

The attorney, with the defendant's consent, filed a motion requesting a settlement conference, tendered an offer to settle for $25,000, and served copies of the motion and tender on the plaintiff's attorney and on the plaintiff personally.

Is the attorney subject to discipline for serving the plaintiff with a copy of the motion and tender?

(A) Yes, unless service of copies of the motion and tender on the plaintiff were authorized by statute or rule of court.

(B) Yes, unless the attorney first informed the plaintiff's attorney of the attorney's intention to serve copies of the motion and tender on the plaintiff.

(C) No, because the decision to accept or reject a settlement offer rests with the client.

(D) No, because the motion and tender became public documents when they were filed in court.

48.

An attorney represents a wife in a marriage dissolution proceeding that involves bitterly contested issues of property division and child custody. After one day of trial, the husband, through his attorney, made a settlement offer. Because of the husband's intense dislike for the attorney, the proposed settlement requires that the attorney agree not to represent the wife in any subsequent proceeding, brought by either party, to modify or enforce the provisions of the decree. The wife wants to accept the offer, and the attorney believes that the settlement offer made by the husband is better than any award the wife would get if the case went to judgment.

Is it proper for the attorney to agree that he will not represent the wife in any subsequent proceeding?

(A) Yes, because the restriction on the attorney is limited to subsequent proceedings in the same matter.

(B) Yes, if the attorney believes that it is in the wife's best interests to accept the proposed settlement.

(C) No, because the proposed settlement would restrict the attorney's right to represent the wife in the future.

(D) No, unless the attorney believes that the wife's interests can be adequately protected by another lawyer in the future.

49.

A company's president telephoned his city's best-known employment attorney and asked her to represent the company in a dispute that had just arisen with the company's chief financial officer. The attorney, who had never previously represented the company, agreed. At the president's insistence, she immediately commenced the representation. A few days later, during a meeting with the president, the attorney first revealed the amount of her customary hourly fee and then explained that the company would also be responsible for reimbursing her expenses. The president responded that her fee was higher than he had expected but that he would be happy for the company to pay it, given her excellent work to date. Although the attorney intended to follow up with a confirming letter, she never did so. For several more months, she assisted the company in resolving its employment dispute. Afterward, she sent the company a bill accurately reflecting her hourly fee and expenses, which were reasonable.

Is the attorney subject to discipline?

(A) Yes, because she did not disclose the basis of her fee before commencing the representation.

(B) Yes, because she did not confirm her fee agreement in writing.

(C) No, because she disclosed the basis of her fee within a reasonable time after commencing the representation.

(D) No, because she was not required to advise the client of her customary hourly fee, unless requested to do so.

50.

In the attorney's closing statement to the court in a bench trial, the attorney said,

> "Your honor, I drive on the street in question every day and I know that a driver cannot see cars backing out of driveways as the one did in this case. I believe that my client was not negligent, and I ask you to so find."

Was the attorney's closing argument proper?

(A) Yes, if the attorney was speaking truthfully and not trying to deceive the court.

(B) Yes, because the rules of evidence are very liberal when the trial is before a judge without a jury.

(C) No, because the attorney asserted her personal knowledge of facts in issue.

(D) No, if there is no other evidence in the record about the facts asserted by the attorney.

51.

A plaintiff who is not a lawyer is representing himself in small claims court in an action to recover his security deposit from his former landlord. The plaintiff told an attorney, a close friend who lived near him, about this case, but did not ask the attorney for any advice. The attorney said,

> "I'll give you some free advice. It would help your case if the new tenants would testify that the apartment was in good shape when they moved in, and, contrary to the allegations of your former landlord, it was not, in fact, repainted for them."

The plaintiff followed the attorney's advice and won his case.

Is the attorney subject to discipline for assisting the plaintiff in preparing for his court appearance?

(A) Yes, because the attorney assisted the plaintiff in the practice of law.

(B) Yes, because the attorney offered unsolicited, in-person legal advice.

(C) No, because the plaintiff was representing himself in the proceedings.

(D) No, because the attorney was not compensated for his advice.

52.

An attorney is defending a client who has been indicted for burglary. During an interview, the client stated to the attorney that before he had consulted the attorney, the client had committed perjury while testifying before the grand jury that indicted him.

The attorney is subject to discipline if she:

(A) continues to represent the client.

(B) continues to represent the client unless he admits his perjury.

(C) does not inform the authorities of the perjury.

(D) informs the authorities of the perjury.

53.

Attorney Alpha, a sole practitioner, recently suffered a heart attack and was advised that she could not return to work for six months. Alpha delivered all of her clients' files to Attorney Beta, who is also a sole practitioner. Beta agreed to review each client's file promptly, take any action necessary to protect each client's interests, and treat the information in the files as confidential. Alpha then wrote her clients, advising each client that the client's file had been delivered to Beta for review and for any action necessary to protect the client's interest, and that the client was free to select another lawyer.

Alpha knows that Beta is a competent attorney. Beta did not accept the file of any person whose interests were, or could be, adverse to the interests of any of Beta's own clients.

Was it proper for Alpha to deliver the files to Beta for review?

(A) Yes, because Alpha knows that Beta is competent to protect the clients' interests.

(B) Yes, because Beta agreed to treat the information in the files as confidential.

(C) Yes, because given her medical condition, Alpha's delivery of the files was necessary to protect the clients' interests.

(D) No, because Alpha did not obtain the prior consent of each client whose file was delivered to Beta.

54.

A judge has recently resigned from the state trial court bench. When she was a judge, she supervised activity in cases pending before another judge while he was on vacation. In one pending case, she entered an administrative order changing the courtroom in which a particular case was to be tried. After trial and appeal, the case was remanded for a new trial. The plaintiff in that case decided to change lawyers and has asked the recently resigned judge to try the case.

Will the judge be subject to discipline if she tries this case on behalf of the plaintiff?

(A) Yes, because the judge acted officially as a judge with respect to an aspect of the case.

(B) Yes, because the judge would try the case before a judge of the court on which she previously sat.

(C) No, because the judge did not act as a judge with respect to a substantial matter in or the merits of the case.

(D) No, because any information that the judge learned about the case while acting as a judge was a matter of public record.

55.

An attorney decided to obtain a master's degree in taxation, but lacked the funds required for tuition and expenses. The attorney consulted one of his clients, a wealthy banker, for advice about obtaining a loan. To the attorney's surprise, the client offered the attorney a personal loan of $10,000. The attorney told the client that he would prepare the required note without charge.

Without further consultation with the client, the attorney prepared and signed a promissory note bearing interest at the current bank rate. The note provided for repayment in the form of legal services to be rendered by the attorney to the client without charge until the value of the attorney's services equaled the principal and interest due. The note further provided that if the client died before the note was fully repaid, any remaining principal and interest would be forgiven as a gift.

The attorney mailed the executed note to the client with a transmittal letter encouraging the client to look it over and call with any questions. The client accepted the note and sent the attorney a personal check for $10,000, which the attorney used to obtain his master's degree. A month after the degree was awarded, the client was killed in a car accident. The attorney had not rendered any legal services to the client from the date of the note's execution to the date of the client's death. Thereafter, in an action brought by the client's estate to recover on the note, the court ruled that the note was discharged as a gift.

Was the attorney's conduct proper?

(A) Yes, because the client, without being requested by the attorney to do so, voluntarily made the loan.

(B) Yes, because the court ruled that the note had been discharged as a gift.

(C) No, because a lawyer may never accept a loan from a client.

(D) No, because the attorney did not comply with the requirements for entering into a business transaction with a client.

56.

An attorney served as a state congressman immediately prior to reopening his law office in the state. The attorney printed and mailed an announcement of his return to private practice to members of the bar, persons who had previously been his clients, and personal friends whom he had never represented. The printed announcement stated that the attorney had reopened his law office, gave his address and telephone number, and added that he had recently served as a state congressman.

Is the attorney subject to discipline for the announcement?

(A) Yes, because it was mailed to persons who had not been his clients.

(B) Yes, because his service as a congressman is unrelated to his ability as a lawyer.

(C) No, because the information in the announcement is true.

(D) No, because all of the information was already in the public domain.

57.

An attorney placed an associate, recently admitted to the bar, in complete charge of the work of the paralegals in the attorney's office. That work consisted of searching titles to real property, an area in which the associate had no familiarity. The attorney instructed the associate to review the searches prepared by the paralegals, and thereafter to sign the attorney's name to the required certifications of title if the associate was satisfied that the search accurately reflected the condition of the title. This arrangement enabled the attorney to lower office operating expenses. The attorney told the associate that the associate should resolve any legal questions that might arise and not to bother the attorney because the attorney was too busy handling major litigation.

Is it proper for the attorney to assign the associate this responsibility?

(A) Yes, if the paralegals are experienced in searching titles.

(B) Yes, because the attorney is ultimately liable for the accuracy of the title searches.

(C) No, unless it enables the attorney to charge lower fees for title certification.

(D) No, because the attorney is not adequately supervising the work of the associate.

58.

A law firm agreed to represent a client in various business matters. The written retainer agreement called for the client to pay hourly rates of $180 per hour for a partner's time and $110 per hour for an associate's time. The representation proceeded and the firm submitted monthly bills, which the client paid promptly, After two years, the firm decided to increase their hourly rates by $10. The firm thereafter billed the client at their new rates, but did not specifically inform the client of the increase. The client continued to pay monthly bills promptly.

Are the firm's partners subject to discipline?

(A) Yes, because the entire original fee agreement was required to be in writing.

(B) Yes, because the client did not consent to the increase.

(C) No, if the $10 hourly increase is reasonable.

(D) No, because the client agreed in writing to pay the firm's hourly rate.

59.

A sole practitioner was appointed to represent a criminal defendant on appeal. A recently admitted lawyer who shared office space with the sole practitioner agreed to write the brief if the sole practitioner would pay him one-half of the statutory fee. The defendant agreed to the arrangement in writing, after full consultation. The recently admitted lawyer entered an appearance as co-counsel for the defendant and, with the sole practitioner's knowledge, applied for and received several extensions of time to file the brief. Subsequently, the appellate court dismissed the appeal for failure to pursue the appeal. A third lawyer was later appointed to represent the defendant, whose conviction was affirmed after the appeal was reinstated.

Is the sole practitioner subject to discipline?

(A) Yes, because he neglected the defendant's case.

(B) Yes, because he shared fees with the recently admitted lawyer.

(C) No, because the defendant agreed in writing to the co-counsel arrangement.

(D) No, because the affirmance by the appellate court indicated that the defendant's appeal was without merit.

60.

An attorney's standard retainer contract in divorce cases provides for the payment of a fee of one-third of the amount of alimony or property settlement secured by the attorney. The attorney declines to represent clients who do not agree to this arrangement.

Is the attorney's standard retainer contract proper?

(A) Yes, because clients often prefer to pay a lawyer a fee based on the outcome of the case.

(B) Yes, if a fee of one-third is not excessive.

(C) No, because a lawyer may not acquire a proprietary interest in a cause of action.

(D) No, because the fee is contingent.

61.

An attorney was retained to represent the client in defense of an action brought against the client by a plaintiff. In order to obtain ample time for settlement negotiations, the attorney immediately requested and obtained from opposing counsel a stipulation extending the client's time to answer the complaint until 10 days after receipt of written demand from the plaintiff's attorney. Four months later, no settlement had been reached, and on May 1, the plaintiff's attorney wrote to the attorney demanding that an answer be filed within 10 days. When no answer was filed by May 15, the plaintiff's attorney had a default judgment entered in favor of the plaintiff.

The attorney was away on a two-month vacation when the plaintiff's attorney's letter was received in her office. When the attorney returned on June 15, she promptly moved to have the default set aside and her motion was granted.

Is the attorney subject to discipline?

(A) Yes, unless she makes restitution to the client for any loss sustained by the client.

(B) Yes, if she did not make provision for the handling of her pending cases while she was away.

(C) No, because the default judgment was set aside.

(D) No, unless she knew that the plaintiff's attorney had demanded that an answer be filed within 10 days.

62.

An attorney represented a plaintiff in an action against a manufacturer of a drain cleaner. The plaintiff's complaint alleged that the manufacturer's product exploded in use and caused her serious and permanent injuries. The jury agreed and awarded the plaintiff $5,000,000 in actual damages and an additional $5,000,000 in punitive damages. The manufacturer paid the judgment.

The attorney made this recovery the cornerstone of an aggressive television advertising campaign for his law practice. In those ads, a voice-over discussed the $10,000,000 recovery obtained in the plaintiff's case. The plaintiff praised the attorney's legal skills in an on-camera statement, saying that no one would work harder on a case than the attorney.

The plaintiff prepared her on-camera statement in response to the attorney's request, but without any further involvement by the attorney, and she believed it to be entirely true.

Is the attorney subject to discipline for using the television advertisement described above?

(A) Yes, because the advertisement is likely to create an unjustified expectation about the results the attorney will be able to achieve and is therefore misleading.

(B) Yes, because the attorney's advertisement contains a client testimonial.

(C) No, because the plaintiff prepared the entire statement without any involvement by the attorney.

(D) No, because the result obtained in the plaintiff's case was reported accurately, and the plaintiff believed that everything she said about the attorney was true.

63.

A corporation hired a law firm to handle all of its corporate work. The firm had not previously represented a corporation on an ongoing basis, but decided that it wanted to attract additional corporate clients. Accordingly, the partners handling the corporation's work began a practice of giving to all lawyers in the firm, on a monthly basis, detailed descriptions of the work they were doing for the corporation for the purpose of illustrating what the firm could do for corporate clients. One of the partners mentioned this practice to the corporation's management, and the corporation complained that its confidences had been violated.

Was it proper for the partners to give detailed descriptions of the work being done for the corporation to other lawyers in the firm?

(A) Yes, because, absent client instructions to the contrary, lawyers may discuss client information with other lawyers in the firm.

(B) Yes, because lawyers may discuss client information with other lawyers in the firm, regardless of client instructions to the contrary, so long as the disclosure does not disadvantage the client.

(C) No, because sharing the information increased the risk that it might be improperly disclosed to third parties outside the firm.

(D) No, because lawyers may not disclose client information, even to other firm lawyers, unless the disclosure is in furtherance of the representation.

64.

An attorney has been representing the client in a matter in litigation. During protracted pretrial proceedings, the client complained bitterly about the time and expense involved and insisted that the attorney take steps to terminate the pretrial proceedings. The attorney believes that to do so would jeopardize the client's interests and has so informed the client. The attorney believes that the case cannot be adequately prepared for trial without further pretrial proceedings that will require an additional six months' delay and involve further expense. The client insists that the attorney forego any further pretrial proceedings and set the case for trial at the earliest available date. There are several other competent lawyers who are willing to undertake the representation.

Is it proper for the attorney to ask leave of the court to withdraw?

(A) Yes, because a lawyer may discontinue representation in a civil case at any time before trial.

(B) Yes, because the client's conduct makes it unreasonably difficult for the attorney to represent the client effectively and competently.

(C) No, because the attorney must follow the client's instructions.

(D) No, unless the client consents to the attorney's withdrawal.

65.

The judicial district in which a judge sits has a rule that allows litigants two postponements as a matter of right. After that, a litigant who moves for a postponement must convince the presiding judge that a postponement is appropriate. The judge routinely grants additional postponements because, in her view,

"What harm is done if one of the litigants wants a postponement? The worst that can happen is that the parties have more time to negotiate and thus are more likely to settle."

Are the judge's actions proper?

(A) Yes, because the judge is exercising her judicial discretion.

(B) Yes, because a party objecting to a postponement can seek appellate review.

(C) No, because judges have no official obligation to encourage private settlements.

(D) No, because the judge should expedite the determination of matters before her.

66.

A trial court judge had instructed his court clerk and his secretary that one of them should be present in the office during working hours to answer the telephone. One day, however, the secretary was out sick. The judge was in his office when his court clerk was at lunch, and when the telephone rang, the judge answered it. The call was from a lawyer in a case presently pending before the judge. The lawyer was calling to attempt to reschedule a pretrial conference set for the next day because of a sudden family emergency. The lawyer had tried to call opposing counsel on the case, but she was not answering his calls. The judge agreed to reschedule the pretrial conference for the following week. When the judge's court clerk returned from lunch, the judge instructed the clerk to contact opposing counsel to inform her of the telephone call and the fact that the pretrial conference had been rescheduled.

Did the judge act properly?

(A) No, because the judge participated in an ex parte communication.

(B) No, because there was still time for the calling lawyer to notify opposing counsel in order to reach agreement on rescheduling the pretrial conference.

(C) Yes, because the ex parte communication was for scheduling purposes only and did not deal with substantive matters or issues.

(D) Yes, because there was no one else in the office to take the lawyer's call.

67.

An attorney, who had represented a client for many years, prepared the client's will and acted as one of the two subscribing witnesses to its execution. The client's sister and brother were his sole heirs. The will left the client's entire estate to his sister and nothing to his brother. Upon the client's death two years later the executor named in the will asked the attorney to act as his lawyer in the probate of the will and the administration of the estate. At that time, the executor informed the attorney that the client's brother would concede that the will was properly executed but intended to contest the will on the ground that he had been excluded because of fraud previously practiced on the client by the client's sister. The other subscribing witness to the will predeceased the client, and the attorney will be called as a witness solely for the purpose of establishing the due execution of the will.

Is it proper for the attorney to accept the representation?

(A) Yes, if there is no contested issue of fact with respect to the formal execution of the will.

(B) Yes, because the executor has no beneficial interest under the will.

(C) No, unless the attorney's services are necessary to avoid substantial hardship to the executor.

(D) No, because the attorney will be called as a witness in the case.

68.

An attorney has been retained to defend an adult charged with a sex offense involving a minor. The attorney believes that, in order to win the case, she must keep parents of minor children off the jury. The attorney instructed her investigator as follows:

"Visit the neighborhood of those prospective jurors on the panel with minor children. Ask the neighbors if they know of any kind of unusual sex activity of the prospective juror or any member of the family. This talk will get back to the prospective jurors, and they will think of excuses not to serve. But don't under any circumstances talk directly with any prospective juror or member of the family."

Is the attorney subject to discipline for so instructing her investigator?

(A) Yes, unless the prospective jurors investigated are, in fact, selected to serve on the jury in the case.

(B) Yes, because the investigation is intended to harass prospective jurors and members of their families.

(C) No, if the matters inquired into might be relevant to a prospective juror's qualifications to serve in the case.

(D) No, because no prospective juror was directly contacted.

69.

A client telephoned an attorney who had previously represented him. The client described a problem on which he needed advice and made an appointment for the following week to discuss the matter with the attorney. Prior to the appointment, the attorney performed five hours of preliminary research on the client's problem. At the end of the appointment the client agreed that the attorney should pursue the matter and agreed to a fee of $100 per hour. The client then gave the attorney a check for $5,000 to cover the five hours already worked and as an advance on additional fees and expenses.

The attorney gave the check to the office bookkeeper with directions to deposit the check into the client trust account and immediately transfer $3,000 to the general office account to cover the five hours of research already conducted plus the 25 additional hours she would spend on the matter the following week. At that time, the attorney reasonably believed that she would spend 25 additional hours on the case.

The bookkeeper followed these directions. The next week, the attorney worked diligently on the matter for 23 hours. Reasonably believing that no significant work remained to be done on the matter, the attorney directed the bookkeeper to transfer $200 from the general office account to the client trust account. The attorney then called the client and made an appointment to discuss the status of the matter.

Is the attorney subject to discipline?

(A) Yes, because the attorney accepted legal fees in advance of performing the work.

(B) Yes, because the attorney transferred funds for unearned fees to the general office account.

(C) No, because the attorney transferred the $200 owed to the client from the general office account to the client trust account.

(D) No, because the attorney reasonably believed that she would spend 25 additional hours on the case.

70.

An attorney represented a plaintiff in an action against several defendants. The retainer agreement provided that the plaintiff would pay all costs and expenses of litigation and would, on demand, reimburse the attorney for any costs or expenses advanced by the attorney. After serving process on two defendants, the attorney had difficulty locating and serving the remaining defendants. The plaintiff approved the hiring of an investigator to locate and serve the defendants, and the attorney advanced the costs for the investigator. When the attorney asked the plaintiff for reimbursement, the plaintiff refused to pay. The attorney then told the plaintiff that the attorney would do no more work on the case until the attorney was reimbursed for the amount advanced.

Thereafter, one of the defendants filed a counterclaim that required a responsive pleading within 30 days. Because the attorney had not been paid, the attorney permitted the time to respond to the counterclaim to expire without filing a responsive pleading, and a default was entered on the counterclaim. Later, the plaintiff reimbursed the attorney for the costs the attorney had advanced, and the attorney was successful in having the default on the counterclaim set aside. The case was tried, and the plaintiff prevailed on the plaintiff's complaint, and the counterclaimant recovered nothing.

Is the attorney subject to discipline for not initially filing a responsive pleading to the counterclaim?

(A) Yes, because the attorney neglected the plaintiff's cause.

(B) Yes, unless the attorney had asked leave of court to withdraw.

(C) No, because the plaintiff breached the agreement to reimburse the attorney.

(D) No, because the plaintiff did not sustain any prejudice as a result of the attorney's action.

71.

A judge, prior to her recent appointment to the federal court, had been an outspoken and effective opponent of the racial segregation policies of a foreign country's government. As part of its worldwide tour, that country's national soccer team scheduled a soccer match with a team in this country. Several civil rights groups have applied to the judge for an order enjoining the playing of the proposed match. The matter is now pending. Only legal issues are presented. The judge, after painstaking consideration, has privately concluded that she cannot decide the legal questions without bias against the representatives of the country's government. However, no one has made a motion to disqualify the judge.

Must the judge recuse herself in the pending matter?

(A) Yes, unless the judge believes she has greater expertise than other judges on the court in legal issues involving racial segregation.

(B) Yes, because the judge believes that she cannot be impartial.

(C) No, because the only issues presented for decision are legal questions.

(D) No, because none of the interested parties has moved to disqualify the judge.

72.

An attorney agreed to represent a plaintiff in a personal injury matter. The original agreement between the attorney and the plaintiff specified a 30 percent contingent fee, which was a reasonable fee for the type of cases the attorney handled. One year into the litigation, the attorney noted that he was extremely busy and that many potential clients sought his services. As a result, the attorney raised his standard fee to a 35 percent contingent fee, which was also a reasonable fee. The attorney's agreement with the plaintiff was silent on the possibility of a fee increase. He approached the plaintiff and proposed that she agree to modify the contingent fee percentage from 30 percent to 35 percent. The attorney informed the plaintiff that if she did not agree, the attorney would find her another experienced personal injury lawyer at the original fee, but that the attorney was unwilling to continue the representation unless the fee was modified. The plaintiff reluctantly agreed to modify the fee agreement as the attorney proposed.

Subsequently, the plaintiff's case was settled. The plaintiff, however, refused to pay the attorney more than a 30 percent contingent fee, and the attorney sued the plaintiff to recover under the modified fee agreement.

Is the attorney likely to prevail?

(A) Yes, because the attorney offered to find the plaintiff another experienced personal injury lawyer at the original rate.

(B) Yes, because a contingent fee of 35 percent constituted a reasonable fee.

(C) No, because the attorney did not suggest that the plaintiff seek the advice of independent counsel before accepting the increased fee.

(D) No, because there were no special circumstances justifying the attorney's insistence on a fee increase.

73.

A member of the bar is a candidate for judicial office in an election. The candidate personally asked several of his friends to contribute $1,000 each to kick off his campaign. After the candidate's friends made the contributions, the candidate, who was elated by the support, formed a committee to collect more contributions. The candidate then turned over the contributions to the committee and began campaigning in earnest.

Is the candidate subject to discipline?

(A) No, because the candidate turned over the funds to his committee.

(B) No, unless the committee includes lawyers likely to practice before the candidate.

(C) Yes, unless none of the original contributors was a lawyer.

(D) Yes, because the candidate personally solicited funds.

74.

An attorney was hired to file a lawsuit against the client's former employer, a corporation, for wrongful discharge. The attorney filed the suit in federal district court based upon three grounds. It turned out that a unanimous U.S. Supreme Court decision had recently eliminated the third ground as a theory available to plaintiffs in wrongful discharge cases. The corporation filed a motion alleging that the complaint was based upon a theory (the third ground) that is no longer supported by existing law and cited the new decision. Within 10 days after the filing of the complaint, the attorney withdrew the third ground and continued with the litigation.

Is the attorney subject to litigation sanction?

(A) Yes, unless the attorney discussed the adverse legal authority with the client before filing the complaint.

(B) Yes, because the client should have cited the U.S. Supreme Court decision in the complaint.

(C) No, because the attorney withdrew the third ground within 10 days after filing the complaint.

(D) No, unless the attorney knew or should have known of the recent decision when the complaint was filed.

75.

Although licensed to practice law in the state, an attorney does not practice law but works as an investment broker. The attorney could have elected inactive status as a member of the bar, but chose not to do so. Recently, in connection with a sale of worthless securities, the attorney made materially false representations to an investment customer.

The customer sued the attorney for civil fraud, and a jury returned a verdict in the customer's favor. The attorney did not appeal.

Is the attorney subject to discipline?

(A) Yes, because the attorney was pursuing a non-legal occupation while an active member of the bar.

(B) Yes, because the attorney's conduct was fraudulent.

(C) No, because the attorney was not convicted of a crime.

(D) No, unless the standard of proof in the state is the same in lawyer disciplinary cases and civil cases.

76.

A client was an experienced oil and gas developer. The client asked an attorney for representation in a suit to establish the client's ownership of certain oil and gas royalties. The client did not have available the necessary funds to pay the attorney's reasonable hourly rate for undertaking the case. The client proposed instead to pay the attorney an amount in cash equal to 20 percent of the value of the proceeds received from the first year royalties the client might recover as a result of the suit. The attorney accepted the proposal and took the case.

Is the attorney subject to discipline?

(A) Yes, because the agreement gave the attorney a proprietary interest in the client's cause of action.

(B) Yes, unless the fee the attorney receives does not exceed that which the attorney would have received by charging a reasonable hourly rate.

(C) No, because the client rather than the attorney proposed the fee arrangement.

(D) No, because the attorney may contract with the client for a reasonable contingent fee.

77.

An attorney has been hired by a client to represent the client in a civil commitment proceeding initiated by the state. The client is now undergoing psychiatric evaluation to determine whether civil commitment should be ordered. The client told the attorney that the client intends to commit suicide as soon as the tests are completed, and the attorney believes that the client will carry out this threat. Suicide and attempted suicide are crimes in the state.

Is it proper for the attorney to disclose the client's intentions to the authorities?

(A) Yes, because the information concerns a future crime and is not protected by the attorney-client evidentiary privilege.

(B) Yes, because the information concerns a future crime that is likely to result in the client's imminent death.

(C) No, unless the attorney knows that the client has attempted suicide in the past.

(D) No, because disclosure would aid the state in its civil commitment case against the client.

78.

An attorney is a long-time member of the state legislature and serves on the legislative budget committee that funds the local trial courts in the state. The attorney also maintains a part-time law practice as is permitted in the state. An influential businessperson who regularly makes significant contributions to the attorney's political campaigns asked the attorney to help his uncle, who was involved in a bitter divorce. The attorney called the trial judge sitting on the uncle's case, a personal friend of the attorney. In discussing some upcoming votes of the budget committee with the judge, the attorney mentioned that the uncle was the type of solid citizen and influential person who could help garner support for the budget and thus ensure the economic health of the judicial system.

Is the attorney subject to discipline?

(A) Yes, if the trial judge ruled in the uncle's favor.

(B) Yes, because the attorney used her public position to attempt to influence a tribunal in a pending matter.

(C) No, if the attorney called the trial judge in her capacity as a legislator and not as the uncle's lawyer.

(D) No, because members of the state legislature are permitted by law to engage in part-time legal practice.

79.

A judge in a criminal trial court of the state wishes to serve as guardian of her father, who has been declared incompetent. Accepting the responsibilities of the position would not interfere with the performance of the judge's official duties. Although the position in all likelihood would not involve contested litigation, it would be necessary for the judge to prepare and sign various pleadings, motions, and other papers and to appear in civil court on her father's behalf.

Would it be proper for the judge to undertake this guardianship?

(A) Yes, unless the judge receives compensation for her services as guardian.

(B) Yes, because the position involves a close family member and will not interfere with the judge's performance of her judicial duties.

(C) No, because the position will require the judge to appear in court.

(D) No, because the position will require the judge to prepare and sign pleadings, motions, and other papers.

80.

An attorney represents a corporation that is a defendant in a product liability case. An engineer who is a corporation employee and nearing retirement was likely to be a key witness in the case, as she had been in charge of all of the corporation's product safety testing during the relevant period. The engineer had been very critical of the corporation's safety testing procedures during that period and had repeatedly complained that the product at issue had not been adequately tested. The engineer's views were reduced to writing and were well known to many employees of the corporation. Because of the early stage of the case, however, plaintiff's counsel was not yet aware of the engineer's existence or her views.

Aware of the engineer's views, the attorney approached the corporation's officials and recommended that it offer the engineer a special package of severance benefits if she would retire immediately and move to the Bahamas. The attorney believed that if the engineer accepted this offer, she would be beyond the subpoena power of the court in which the suit against the corporation was pending. The corporation adopted the attorney's recommendation and made the offer. The engineer accepted it. The attorney did not disclose the engineer's identity to plaintiff's counsel.

Is the attorney subject to discipline?

(A) Yes, because the attorney caused the engineer to leave the jurisdiction of the court for the purpose of making her unavailable as a witness.

(B) Yes, because opposing counsel had not yet had a reasonable opportunity to learn of the engineer's views.

(C) No, because the engineer's views were reduced to writing and are well known to many other employees of the corporation.

(D) No, unless there was a pending request for the engineer's testimony at the time the retirement offer was made to the engineer.

81.

An attorney represented a client in a personal injury action against the driver of the car in which the client was injured while a passenger. The personal injury action was settled, and the attorney received a check in the amount of $10,000 payable to the attorney. The attorney deposited the check in her Clients' Trust Account.

One day later, the attorney received a letter from a bank that had heard of the settlement of the personal injury lawsuit. The bank informed the attorney that the client had failed to make his monthly mortgage payments for the last three months and demanded that the attorney immediately release $900 of the proceeds of the settlement to the bank or the bank would institute mortgage foreclosure proceedings against the client. The attorney informed the client of the bank's letter. The client responded:

"I don't care what the bank does. The property is essentially worthless, so let the bank foreclose. If the bank wants to sue me, I'll be easy enough to find. I don't think they'll even bother. You just take your legal fees and turn the rest of the proceeds over to me."

Is the attorney subject to discipline if she follows the client's instructions?

(A) Yes, if the client does not dispute the $900 debt to the bank.

(B) Yes, because the attorney knew that the client was planning to force the bank to sue him.

(C) No, unless the attorney had reason to believe that the client would not have sufficient funds to pay any subsequent judgment obtained by the bank.

(D) No, because the bank has no established right to the specific proceeds of the client's personal injury judgment.

82.

Three lawyers, Alpha, Beta, and Delta, formed a partnership to practice law with offices in both State First and State Second. Alpha is admitted to practice only in State First. Beta is admitted to practice only in State Second, and Delta is admitted to practice in both States First and Second. The following letterhead is on stationery used by their offices in both states:

Alpha, Beta, and Delta

Attorneys at Law

100 State Street	200 Bank Building
City, State First	City, State Second
(200) 555-5555	(202) 555-5555

Attorney Alpha

Admitted to practice only

in State First

Attorney Beta

Admitted to practice only

in State Second

Attorney Delta

Admitted to practice

in States First and Second

Are the members of the partnership subject to discipline?

(A) No, because the letterhead states the jurisdictions in which each partner is admitted.

(B) Yes, because there is no jurisdiction in which both Alpha and Beta are admitted to practice.

(C) Yes, because the firm name used by each office contains the name of a lawyer not admitted to practice in that jurisdiction.

(D) Yes, unless Delta actively practices law in both States First and Second.

83.

An attorney was engaged under a general retainer agreement to represent a corporation involved in the uranium industry. Under the agreement, the attorney handled all of the corporation's legal work, which typically involved regulatory issues and litigation.

The corporation told the attorney that a congressional committee was holding hearings concerning the extent of regulation in the copper industry. Because the corporation was considering buying a copper mine during the next fiscal year, the corporation wanted the attorney to testify that the industry was overregulated. The attorney subsequently testified before the relevant congressional committee. The attorney registered his appearance under his own name and did not disclose that he was appearing on behalf of a client. Afterward, the attorney billed the corporation for fees and expenses related to his testimony.

Was the attorney's conduct proper?

(A) Yes, because the duty of confidentiality prevented the attorney from disclosing the identity of his client.

(B) Yes, because the attorney-client evidentiary privilege prevented disclosure of the identity of his client in this context.

(C) No, because the attorney failed to disclose that he was appearing and testifying in a representative capacity.

(D) No, because the attorney accepted compensation in return for his testimony.

84.

An attorney represented a man in a case set for a jury trial. After the list of potential jurors was made available, the attorney hired a private investigator to interview the potential jurors and their family members concerning their relevant past experiences related to the subject matter of the action. The investigator did not inform the jurors or their family members that he was working on behalf of the attorney. The interviews were entirely voluntary and were not harassing.

The attorney did not provide the report of the interviews to opposing counsel. He used the report to make decisions regarding jury selection.

Is the attorney subject to discipline?

(A) Yes, because the attorney did not provide the report of the interviews to opposing counsel.

(B) Yes, because the investigator, at the attorney's direction, communicated with potential jurors prior to trial.

(C) Yes, because the investigator did not inform the jurors or their family members that he was working on behalf of the attorney.

(D) No, because the interviews were entirely voluntary and not harassing.

85.

For many years, an attorney has served as outside counsel to a corporation. Shortly after a change in management, the attorney discovered what she reasonably believed to be a material misstatement in a document she had drafted that the attorney was about to file on the corporation's behalf with a government agency. The attorney advised the corporation's board of directors that filing the document was probably criminal. However, the board disagreed that there was any material misstatement and directed the attorney to proceed with the filing. When the attorney indicated her intention to resign, the corporation argued that a resignation at this time would send a signal that there was a problem with the filing. The corporation urged the attorney to continue the representation, but offered to use in-house counsel to complete the work on the filing. Although she does not know for certain that filing the document is illegal, the attorney reasonably believes that it is. In any event, the attorney is personally uncomfortable with the representation and wants to withdraw.

May the attorney withdraw from her representation of the corporation?

(A) Yes, because withdrawal is permitted but not required when a client insists on conduct which the lawyer reasonably believes, but does not know, will be criminal.

(B) Yes, because withdrawal is required when a client insists on conduct which the lawyer reasonably believes, but does not know, will be criminal.

(C) No, if the corporation is correct that withdrawal would breach confidentiality by sending a signal that the filing is problematic.

(D) No, if the attorney's withdrawal as outside counsel might affect the corporation's ability to complete the filing in a timely fashion.

86.

A judge and an attorney were formerly law partners. During their partnership, they acquired several parcels of real property as co-tenants. After the judge was elected to the trial court in the county, she remained a co-tenant with the attorney, but left the management of the properties to the attorney.

The judge's term of office will expire soon and she is opposed for reelection by two members of the bar. The attorney, who has not discussed the matter with the judge, intends to make a substantial contribution to the judge's campaign for reelection.

The judge is one of 15 judges sitting as trial court judges in the county.

Is the attorney subject to discipline if the attorney contributes $10,000 to the judge's reelection campaign?

(A) Yes, if the attorney frequently represents clients in cases tried in the trial court of the county.

(B) Yes, because the judge and the attorney have not discussed the matter of a campaign contribution.

(C) No, if the contribution is made to a campaign committee organized to support the judge's reelection.

(D) No, because the attorney and the judge have a long-standing personal and business relationship.

87.

Attorney Alpha, a partner in the law firm of Alpha & Beta, was retained by the plaintiff in a personal injury action against the defendant. The jury rendered a verdict in favor of the defendant, and Alpha filed an appeal on the plaintiff's behalf. Alpha reviewed the trial transcript and wrote the brief. The brief stated, "It is uncontroverted that the defendant failed to signal before turning left into the intersection." In fact, a witness called by the defendant testified that the defendant did signal before turning. Alpha was aware of this testimony, having read it while reviewing the trial transcript.

Three days before the appeal was scheduled to be argued in the state's intermediate appellate court, Alpha suffered a heart attack. Attorney Beta, one of Alpha's partners, agreed to argue the appeal. Beta knew nothing about the case and had no opportunity to confer with Alpha. In preparing for the argument, Beta read Alpha's brief thoroughly and read as much of the trial transcript as was possible in the limited time available, but did not read the witness's testimony. In oral argument, Beta stated to the court, "Your honors, as stated in our brief, it is uncontroverted that the defendant failed to signal before turning left into the intersection." Beta assumed that Alpha's statement in the brief to that effect was correct.

Is Beta subject to discipline for making this statement during oral argument?

(A) Yes, because the statement was false.

(B) Yes, because Beta did not know whether or not the statement was true.

(C) No, because Beta did not know that the statement was false.

(D) No, because all Beta did was to truthfully recount the statement made by Alpha in the brief.

88.

A judge needed to obtain a loan to be secured by a second mortgage on his house. A bank offered him a loan at a very favorable interest rate. The vice-president at the bank told the judge:

"Frankly, we normally don't give such a large loan when the security is a second mortgage, and your interest rate will be 2 percent less than we charge our other customers. But we know that your salary is inadequate, and we are giving you special consideration."

Is it proper for the judge to accept the loan?

(A) Yes, if the judge does not act in any case involving the bank.

(B) Yes, if the bank is not likely to be involved in litigation in the court on which the judge sits.

(C) No, unless the same terms are available to all judges in the state.

(D) No, because the amount of the loan and interest rate were not available to persons who were not judges.

89.

A law firm has 300 lawyers in 10 states. It has placed the supervision of all routine administrative and financial matters in the hands of a non-lawyer. The non-lawyer is paid a regular monthly salary and a year-end bonus of 1 percent of the law firm's net income from fees. Organizationally, the non-lawyer reports to an attorney who acts as the managing partner of the law firm. The attorney deals with all issues related to the law firm's supervision of the practice of law.

Is it proper for the attorney to participate in the law firm's use of the non-lawyer's services in this fashion?

(A) Yes, unless the non-lawyer has access to client files.

(B) Yes, if the non-lawyer does not control the professional judgment of the lawyers in the firm.

(C) No, because the law firm is sharing legal fees with a non-lawyer.

(D) No, because the law firm is assisting a non-lawyer in the unauthorized practice of law.

90.

An attorney experienced several instances when clients failed to pay their fees in a timely manner, but it was too late in the representation to withdraw without prejudicing the clients. To avoid a recurrence of this situation, the attorney has drafted a stipulation of consent to withdraw if fees are not paid according to the fee agreement. She proposes to have all clients sign the stipulation at the outset of the representation.

Is it proper for the attorney to use the stipulation to withdraw from representation whenever a client fails to pay fees?

(A) Yes, because a lawyer may withdraw when the financial burden of continuing the representation would be substantially greater than the parties anticipated at the time of the fee agreement.

(B) Yes, because the clients consented to the withdrawal in the stipulation.

(C) No, because a client's failure to pay fees when due may be insufficient in itself to justify withdrawal.

(D) No, unless clients are provided an opportunity to seek independent legal advice before signing the stipulation.

91.

An attorney was retained by a client to represent him in a paternity suit. The client's aunt believed the suit was unfounded and motivated by malice. The client's aunt sent the attorney a check for $1,000 and asked the attorney to apply it to the payment of the client's fee. The client's aunt told the attorney not to tell the client of the payment because the client "is too proud to accept gifts, but I know he really needs the money."

Is it proper for the attorney to accept the aunt's check?

(A) Yes, if the client's aunt does not attempt to influence the attorney's conduct of the case.

(B) Yes, if the attorney's charges to the client are reduced accordingly.

(C) No, because the client's aunt is attempting to finance litigation to which she is not a party.

(D) No, unless the attorney first informs the client and obtains the client's consent to retain the payment.

92.

An attorney has a highly efficient staff of paraprofessional legal assistants, all of whom are graduates of recognized legal assistant educational programs. Recently, the statute of limitations ran against a claim of a client of the attorney's when a legal assistant negligently misplaced a client's file and suit was not filed within the time permitted by law.

Which of the following correctly states the attorney's professional responsibility?

(A) The attorney is subject to civil liability and is also subject to discipline on the theory of respondeat superior.

(B) The attorney is subject to civil liability or is subject to discipline at the client's election.

(C) The attorney is subject to civil liability but is NOT subject to discipline unless the attorney failed to supervise the legal assistant adequately.

(D) The attorney is NOT subject to civil liability and is NOT subject to discipline if the attorney personally was not negligent.

93.

A seller was engaged in negotiations to sell his interest in a large tract of land to a buyer who was unrepresented in the transaction. Before the seller went out of town for a few days, he told the buyer to call his attorney if the buyer had any questions about the property. The buyer called the seller's attorney, asked certain questions about the size of the tract, and expressed hesitations concerning the high asking price for the tract. The attorney responded that, based on his experience handling real estate transactions in the neighborhood, the buyer would be getting a lot of property for the price. At the time the attorney spoke to the buyer, the attorney knew that there was a defect in the title and that the buyer's attempt to purchase the seller's interest in the tract would not result in the buyer's acquisition of any interest in the property.

Relying on the attorney's assurance, the buyer agreed to make the purchase. Shortly after the sale closed, the buyer discovered that his acquisition was worthless.

Is the attorney subject to civil liability to the buyer?

(A) Yes, because the attorney knowingly made false representations of fact to the buyer.

(B) Yes, because the attorney implied that his opinion regarding the value of the property was a disinterested opinion.

(C) No, because the attorney's statement that the buyer would be getting a lot of property for the money was a statement of opinion regarding the value of the property.

(D) No, because the buyer was not a client of the attorney.

94.

A prosecutor was assigned to try a criminal case against a defendant who was charged with robbery of a convenience store. The defendant denied any involvement, contending he was home watching television with his mother on the night in question. At the trial, a customer at the convenience store testified that he had identified the defendant in a police line-up and provided other testimony connecting the defendant to the crime. In addition, the prosecutor entered into evidence a poor-quality videotape of the robbery as recorded by the store surveillance camera. The jury convicted the defendant of the crime charged. Unknown to the defendant's court-appointed lawyer, the customer had first identified another person in the police line-up and selected the defendant only after encouragement by the detective. The prosecutor was aware of these facts but did not notify the defendant's counsel who made no pretrial discovery request to obtain this information.

Is the prosecutor subject to discipline?

(A) Yes, unless the jury could make its own identification of the defendant from the videotape.

(B) Yes, because this information tended to negate the defendant's guilt.

(C) No, because the defendant's counsel made no pretrial discovery request to obtain this information.

(D) No, unless it is likely that the jury would have acquitted the defendant had it known that the customer first identified someone else.

95.

An attorney and a client entered into a written retainer and hourly fee agreement that required the client to pay $5,000 in advance of any services rendered by the attorney and which required the attorney to return any portion of the $5,000 that was not earned. The agreement further provided that the attorney would render monthly statements and withdraw her fees as billed. The agreement was silent as to whether the $5,000 advance was to be deposited in the attorney's Clients' Trust Account or in a general account. The attorney deposited the entire fund in her Clients' Trust Account, which also contained the funds of other persons which had been entrusted to the attorney. Thereafter, the attorney rendered monthly progress reports and statements for services to the client after services were rendered, showing the balance of the client's fee advance. However, the attorney did not withdraw any of the $5,000 advance until one year later when the matter was concluded to the client's complete satisfaction. At that time, the attorney had billed the client reasonable legal fees of $4,500. The attorney wrote two checks on her Clients' Trust Account: one to herself for $4,500, which she deposited in her general office account, and one for $500 to the client.

Was the attorney's conduct proper?

(A) Yes, because the attorney deposited the funds in her Clients' Trust Account.

(B) Yes, because the attorney rendered periodic and accurate billings.

(C) No, because the attorney's failure to withdraw her fees as billed resulted in an impermissible commingling of her funds and the clients' funds.

(D) No, because the attorney required an advanced payment against her fee.

96.

Attorneys Alpha and Beta had been political opponents. Alpha was elected to the state legislature after a bitter race in which Beta had managed the campaign of Alpha's opponent. Alpha had publicly blamed Beta at that time for what Alpha reasonably believed were illegal and unethical campaign practices and later had publicly objected to Beta's appointment as a judge.

Alpha represented a client in a widely publicized case tried in Judge Beta's court. At the conclusion of the trial, Beta ruled against Alpha's client. Alpha then held a press conference and said "All that you reporters have to do is check your files and you will know what I think about Judge Beta's character and fitness."

Is Alpha subject to discipline for making this statement?

(A) Yes, if Alpha's statement might lessen confidence in the legal system.

(B) Yes, because Alpha's past accusations were unrelated to Beta's legal knowledge.

(C) No, because Alpha reasonably believed that the statements about Beta were true.

(D) No, if Beta had equal access to the press.

Answer Key to Sample Questions

1.	B	25.	A	49.	C	73.	D
2.	B	26.	A	50.	C	74.	C
3.	B	27.	B	51.	C	75.	B
4.	C	28.	A	52.	D	76.	D
5.	C	29.	B	53.	D	77.	B
6.	D	30.	A	54.	C	78.	B
7.	D	31.	C	55.	D	79.	B
8.	A	32.	B	56.	C	80.	A
9.	A	33.	A	57.	D	81.	D
10.	C	34.	D	58.	B	82.	A
11.	D	35.	C	59.	A	83.	C
12.	A	36.	C	60.	D	84.	B
13.	D	37.	B	61.	B	85.	A
14.	C	38.	D	62.	A	86.	C
15.	C	39.	D	63.	A	87.	C
16.	D	40.	B	64.	B	88.	D
17.	D	41.	B	65.	D	89.	B
18.	D	42.	B	66.	C	90.	C
19.	D	43.	A	67.	A	91.	D
20.	B	44.	B	68.	B	92.	C
21.	C	45.	A	69.	B	93.	A
22.	A	46.	C	70.	A	94.	B
23.	B	47.	A	71.	B	95.	C
24.	B	48.	C	72.	D	96.	C